# Durga / Umayi

# Durga / Umayi

**A NOVEL**

Y. B. Mangunwijaya

Translated by Ward Keeler

UNIVERSITY OF WASHINGTON PRESS
*Seattle and London*

in association with

SINGAPORE UNIVERSITY PRESS

University of Washington Press
P.O. Box 50096
Seattle, Washington 98145-5096
www.washington.edu/uwpress

ISBN 0-295-98392-2

Cataloging-in-Publication Data can be obtained from
the Library of Congress

Singapore University Press, an imprint
of NUS Publishing
31 Lower Kent Ridge Road
Yusof Ishak House
Singapore 119078
Fax: 65-67740652
supbooks@nus.edu.sg
www.nus.edu.sg/sup

ISBN 9971-69-297-X

*As a token of respect*
*and gratitude to my first teacher of literature,*
*Dr. H. B. Jassin*

# Contents

# Translator's Introduction

Y. B. Mangunwijaya, an Indonesian Catholic priest, engineer, architect, essayist, and public intellectual, wrote several novels. Of them, *Durga/Umayi* is the most original and provocative in both content and form. It provides rich insight into Indonesia's current condition by evoking shared stories about the country's mythical and historical past. This intertwining of past and present enables Mangunwijaya to suggest alternative, critical readings of both. But he does so in a refreshingly irreverent way, making this novel an unusually entertaining and instructive way for people from other places to gain insights into Indonesia's recent history and ongoing predicaments.

Because Mangunwijaya wrote the novel for an Indonesian audience, three matters to which he refers require some explanation for non-Indonesian readers. These are shadow plays, language, and Indonesia's modern history.

Shadow plays are an ancient but still both prestigious and popular art form, consisting of all-night performances in which a puppeteer sits in front of a white screen manipulating flat, intricately cut leather puppets. A bright light above his head casts shadows on the screen: spectators watch either these shadows from behind the screen or the colorfully painted puppets themselves from behind the puppeteer and the gamelan orchestra arrayed around him. A familiar cast of characters and stories based on the Indian epics *Ramayana* and *Mahabharata* recur in all the performances people see in the course of their lives—and if they have any taste for the genre they will have many opportunities to see performances, since they are held in honor of weddings, births, circumcisions, funerals, the opening of new buildings, the founding of new organizations, and so forth.

At the beginning of each chapter of *Durga / Umayi* there appears the image of some familiar shadow play character, bringing immediate associations to the mind of Javanese readers of the novel. (Javanese make up the largest and most powerful ethnic group in Indonesia, constituting about 60 percent of the population. Mangunwijaya himself was ethnic Javanese.) All of the characters in shadow plays are stock types, such as aristocratic knights, rough monsters, demure maidens, and bumpkinish servants. Yet many of them are so familiar and highly individuated that they have the vivid, living quality of characters in a novel. Similarly, the characters in Mangunwijaya's novel are all stereotypes but so vividly drawn that one feels their specific personality immediately. At the same time, by referring to the shadow play tradition in a novel that focuses not on ancient epics but rather on very commonly known and recent events and people, Mangunwijaya gives the novel a remarkably evocative—if often ironic—depth.

One story in particular is evoked throughout the novel. The god Lord Guru (Siva) was riding on the back of the bull Andini one day in the company of his beautiful wife, Umayi, when the rays of the sun caused her to appear particularly lovely, arousing the god's passion. But the goddess, scandalized by her husband's intention of making love before the eyes of the world, rebuffed him. Guru's arousal was beyond restraint, however, and his semen fell into the sea. In his wrath, Guru cursed his wife to take on a monstrous appearance. He banished her to live in the horrific Corpstenchfield and obliged her to marry the monster, Kala, that his seed generated. Her name, in this her monstrous form, became Durga, and the goddess's two names, Durga and Umayi, give the novel its title. The ambiguous status of the goddess's identity, beautiful and monstrous, paragon of virtue and icon of female danger, both somehow present in a single but bifurcated being, sums up the contradictions in the novel's multi-named but single protagonist, Iin (aka Linda Nussy Nusamusbida, etc., names she uses "according to the situation and mood").

This story of Guru and Umayi is performed as part of a ritual use of shadow plays in Java, to rid children suffering under the threat of some ill fate. The threat is occasioned by inauspicious circumstances, such as when children are born twins, as are the novel's protagonist and her brother. Mangunwijaya opens the novel with a dense, allusive prose poem relating this story (although he includes a detail, in which Umayi in turn curses her husband to a monstrous appearance, which is little known in Java but present in ancient Javanese literature and is well known in Bali, the island immediately east of Java). He can give his version of the myth such obscure expression in part because he can count on his readers to know the story at least in outline. He recounts the story's beginning once again, in Chapter Three, when Iin first wonders whether by slicing off the head of a Gurkha soldier she has turned into a Durga herself.

A second reference in the novel is to language, that is, both to the various languages spoken in Indonesia and to stylistic variation within any one language. The seventy million or so native speakers of Javanese speak a language with a highly differentiated set of speech registers. These work somewhat like the distinction between *tu* and *vous* in French, but much more pervasively, affecting all parts of speech. This means that the vocabulary one uses every time one says anything in Javanese depends on the relative status of oneself and the person one is addressing, further modulated according to the tenor of one's relationship to that person and the mood of the moment. Nationalists in the 1920s decided to rename Malay, long the lingua franca of the islands of Southeast Asia, Indonesian and make it the national language of the country they hoped to found once the Dutch colonialists could be persuaded or obliged to leave the Dutch East Indies. The Dutch themselves had decided in the nineteenth century that Malay, once adequately regularized and spruced up, should become the official language of the colonies, reserving knowledge of Dutch for themselves and a few very high-status indigenous aristocrats. Indonesian nationalists shared Dutch prejudices against "Market Malay," a vulgar hodgepodge in their view, and to this day the Indonesian government promotes a "good and correct" version of Indonesian, distant from the everyday speech of native speakers of Malay and of the people in Jakarta who speak the language as their mother tongue. Most Indonesians, including Javanese, still learn Indonesian in school long after they have acquired a regional language (such as Javanese, but there are hundreds of others in Indonesia) as their first one. At the same time, Indonesian as spoken and especially as written by educated Indonesians increasingly takes on the vocabulary and even grammatical structures of English, while Arabic vocabulary proliferates among the increasingly influential reformist Muslims in the country.

Mangunwijaya, instead of rejecting any of the various styles available in contemporary Indonesian, happily uses them all, formulating an altogether unique, zany style that is without precedent in Indonesian or Javanese literature. Chapter One of the novel opens with a parody of the sententious, grandiloquent pontifications, including a dig at "Market Malay," with which Indonesian intellectuals have long sought to make themselves appear important. Indeed, the first paragraph simply doesn't read, because the many learned digressions and interpolations can't make up for the fact that there is no main clause. But this puffed-up style soon gives way to something more down home. Much of the novel is written in free indirect discourse; in these passages, as we listen in on the thoughts of particular characters, we hear everyday Javanese translated into everyday Indonesian. (Virtually all of the characters are of Javanese origin, and Mangunwijaya reminds us of that fact in many references both to places and to features of the Javanese language that come through in the Indonesian he writes.) At other points we are overhearing conversations, and these reproduce stylistic mannerisms of various sorts: the officiousness of the bureaucrat, the bravado of the rebel youth, the pretentious cosmopolitanism of the modern businessman. The stylistic variation makes for hilarious swings from high to low and back, with never a pause. Indeed, the most important stylistic feature of the book is its breathless speed. Although the initial prose poem and the opening of the first chapter are daunting, soon the rhythm of the narration takes on a compulsive, even frenetic, pace.

Mangunwijaya imparts this quality to the writing in part by the action-packed story line. But he does so as well by a kind of grammatical adventurism. That is, he makes indiscriminate use of grammatical structures available in Western languages at some points, and Austronesian (including Indonesian) ones at others. This eclectic approach to grammar enables him to write improbably long sentences with barely a cadence till the end of each chapter. The effect is to convey the headlong, careening quality of what is his main topic and the third set of references central to the novel: modern Indonesian history.

Mangunwijaya uses a simple conceit to convey his version of Indonesian history. He places his protagonist in the thick of many of the events that have formed, and torn at, the country since the 1930s. To appreciate the novelty of his rendering of these events, a reader needs to know their basic outline.

The first chapter of the novel focuses on the period just before Indonesia's independence. The East Indies had been colonized by the Dutch for centuries, but when Japanese invaded in 1942, they quickly took control. Like many other Southeast Asians suddenly freed from Western colonial regimes, Javanese reacted at first enthusiastically to Japanese appeals for solidarity among Asians in opposition to Western imperialism. Before long, however, Javanese became disenchanted with their new rulers, whose brutality and extortionist demands for labor and supplies far exceeded any they had experienced under the Dutch. Many people, including Sukarno and other important nationalist leaders who had gained prominence in the 1930s for their opposition to the Dutch colonial regime, now found themselves faced with a conundrum: to what extent should they collaborate with the Japanese and to what extent should they oppose them? Sukarno and Muhammad Hatta, another nationalist leader, collaborated, while Sutan Syahrir refused. But Sukarno's reputation, founded on his extraordinary oratorical skills and manly good looks, was never tarnished in the eyes of his millions of supporters, especially among masses of Javanese and Balinese peasants. At the same time, Japanese military training of *seinendan* (youth groups) and *heiho* (paramilitary forces) prepared many men for the later fight against the Dutch. In the novel, the varying arrangements and accommodations people made with both Dutch and Japanese colonialism are figured in Iin's ancestors', father's, and mother's consistently opportunistic relations to indigenous Javanese, Dutch and Japanese authorities, while Sukarno's vast charisma shows in Iin's infatuation with his image from the moment she sees it on a movie screen.

The magnetic Sukarno and the more intellectual, modest, and devout Sumatran, Mohammad Hatta, engaged in careful negotiations with Japanese officials as the fate of Japan's imperial venture grew clear in the course of 1945. They were anxious to foster impressions of Indonesia's legitimacy as an independent state. Still they were fearful of overstepping bounds in such a way as to provoke Japanese reprisals at a time when Japanese still maintained control of military power in the region. Younger Indonesian nationalist fighters were much less patient, and out of frustration—and hotheadedness—they kidnapped the two leaders in August 1945, forcing them to declare the country's independence on August 17, 1945. The date, 17–8–1945 in Indonesian rendering, has imbued those numbers with a magical aura. Important Indonesian documents are often designed to have that many sections or pages in order to partake of the numbers' potency, a habit Mangunwijaya happily mocks.

A question that nationalist struggle and the hardships of the Japanese occupation had prevented people from considering seriously was just what sort of society the newly proclaimed Indonesia would be. Would it address the needs of millions of poor peasants living in the archipelago, or would it simply perpetuate patterns of privilege and exploitation long extant in the region, particularly in Java, and further exaggerated and rigidified under the Dutch—with the one change that now indigenous instead of foreign individuals would lord it over all others? In the second chapter of the novel, Mangunwijaya recounts the well-known story of Indonesia's precipitous Proclamation of Independence by placing Iin in domestic service at the house, 56 East Pegangsaan Street, where Sukarno was living in Jakarta at the time. He dramatizes the question of who was to benefit from the country's creation in the surreal figure of the personified microphone in which Iin can voice the aspirations of her downtrodden but now hope-filled class.

The Dutch were not ready to relinquish control of their Southeast Asian colonies, and as soon as they had recovered enough from their own suffering at the hands of the Germans, they tried to reassert control over the islands they still expected to rule. Fighting took place intermittently from 1946 to 1950, with fitful efforts at negotiation going on much of the time. The Javanese court city of Yogyakarta served as the Republic's capital during those years. Fighting for Indonesian independence were both soldiers trained in the Dutch colonial army (the KNIL) and irregulars, youths with little or no military training but great enthusiasm. The division between the more professional fighters and the humbler, more impetuous but undisciplined youths left a lasting tension that took many years to sort out once independence was attained. Fighting on behalf of the Dutch, meanwhile, were other indigenous soldiers still willing to fight in the KNIL, Allied forces ready at the outset of the struggle to support Dutch efforts to return to the Indies, foreign mercenaries, and Dutch soldiers sent out from Europe. As in so many decolonizing wars of the twentieth century, guerrilla warfare was chaotic, brutalizing, and terribly disruptive to civilians' lives. Mangunwijaya's heroine shows herself as committed and daring as any of the guerilla fighters she helps, in Chapter Three, but her experiences prove disillusioning and deeply scarring.

Once Indonesian independence received international recognition, the country set about the task of establishing its place in the world and creating a viable form of government for itself. Sukarno's popularity remained immense in Java and Bali, and he delighted in playing the role of international spokesperson for the anticolonialist "New Emerging Forces" he saw arising in Asia and Africa. Many Indonesians outside Java and Bali grew disenchanted, however, with Jakarta's control, and rebellions started in the mid-fifties that took several years to put down. Sukarno's regime was characterized by ever-increasing corruption and economic disarray. Indeed, Sukarno seems never to have reached a reasoned economic policy in his own mind. Fostering indigenous cooperatives, nationalizing Dutch-owned businesses, printing money—all these measures were taken out of political expediency, with unforeseen and disastrous economic consequences. The disciplined, even ascetic, Hatta was sidelined. The army grew rich on economic ventures of its own. Sukarno took a series of wives. The mass of Indonesia's poor got poorer, while a tiny elite got rich. Iin's morally feckless and complacent accumulation of wealth through sexual and commercial machinations in Chapter Four exemplifies this period, and indeed, all of modern Indonesian history inasmuch as it has been characterized by thoroughgoing corruption.

By the late 1950s, Sukarno had ended Indonesia's efforts to implement parliamentary democracy, replacing it with "Guided Democracy" and grand oratory, including an ever-increasing number of propagandistic formulas of his devising. But in the early 1960s, while he pursued various foreign ventures—engaging in confrontational posturing toward Malaysia and a campaign to incorporate West Irian (western New Guinea) into Indonesia—domestic politics turned increasingly fractious. Many in the military became impatient with Sukarno's treatment of them, and military factions and religious groups felt increasingly threatened by Sukarno's apparent inclination to favor the Indonesian Communist Party over other parties, even his own Indonesian Nationalist Party. The Communist Party (the PKI) came to enjoy immense popularity and was smaller in size only than those in the Soviet Union and China. A great many organizations were set up by the party or were at least linked to it in people's minds. (One such organization was the Indonesian Women's Movement, or Gerwani, although it was never formally affiliated with the PKI despite its leftist perspective.) For the most part, the PKI's platform was diffusely socialist and nationalist rather than doctrinally pure. Intellectuals, however, fought passionately over ideological matters. The dispute over whether "universal humanism" or "socialist realism" provided the better criteria with which to assess aesthetic endeavors was particularly heated, pitting members of the PKI's cultural affairs organization, the Institute of People's Culture (Lekra), against many other established authors and artists. Some prominent figures in the arts issued a "Cultural Manifesto" in 1963 to counter Lekra's claim that an artist's responsibility was to champion the interests of the masses, and recollections of that controversy continue to generate animosity among Indonesian intellectuals to the present.

Catastrophic inflation, an increasingly factionalized military, religious organizations made anxious by the Communists' expanding power and prestige, and some radical "unilateral actions" encouraged by the PKI, in which poor farmers tried to wrest land from other, wealthier neighbors, all generated immense tension that culminated in cataclysmic civil upheaval in 1965 and 1966. The trigger was an army officers' coup against certain of their superiors in Jakarta on September 30, 1965, in which six generals were killed and their bodies thrown into a well, the "Crocodile Hole" at Halim Air Force Base. General Suharto, head of the Army Strategic Reserve in Jakarta, quickly took control, crushing the coup within a few days and then over the following months easing Sukarno out of power, obliging him to sign a document named "Supersemar" in March 1966, in which Sukarno was represented as requesting Suharto to take charge. Meanwhile, the provinces of Central and East Java, Bali, and West Sumatra became scenes of horrific violence. Hundreds of thousands of Communists, or those said to be sympathetic to the PKI—people who had joined organizations enjoying official favor until September 30, 1965—were massacred by the military, Muslim youths, PNI sympathizers, or others who saw an opportunity to exact revenge from their enemies. It was as though something as mainstream as membership in the Democratic Party in the United States suddenly became sufficient grounds for people's summary execution. Hundreds of thousands more people were imprisoned without trial. Eventually, many prisoners were transferred to concentration camps on the island of Buru, in eastern Indonesia, where those who survived the wretched conditions and forced labor lived in legal limbo for many years. The last prisoners, still never having been tried, were released from Buru in 1979, in part due to President Carter's pressure on the Indonesian government.

Most Indonesian authors, like most Indonesians generally, have avoided discussing the nightmarish events of the 1960s except in the highly conventionalized official formulas that demonize all leftists and praise Suharto and the "New Order" regime he founded for restoring order out of chaos. Mangunwijaya, however, describes the passions and absurdities of the early 1960s in Chapter Five, in which Iin plays the socially committed but naïve leftist to the measured and generous Balinese artist Rohadi. And in Chapter Six, Mangunwijaya represents the agonies of the survivors, people who must live with the unintended consequences of their youthful actions, when Iin learns of Rohadi's fate. In the extreme measures Iin must then take to assure her own safety after the coup's suppression, we see the effects of the New Order's vicious persecution of all those who turned out to have chosen the wrong side during Indonesia's fateful second decade.

On gaining power, Suharto immediately went about replacing a vaguely socialist, cooperative-based economic policy meant to foster indigenous business with an American-inspired approach relying on huge infusions of foreign capital. Indonesia's integration into the world capitalist economy quickly created vast fortunes for a new, well-connected military and commercial elite. It also gave rise to a much larger middle class than Indonesia had ever known, and the country enjoyed a remarkably high growth rate for many years. But the rising tide also generated glaring disparities in wealth, something that was thought to have been much less prevalent in the generalized poverty of the past.

The New Order reimagined Indonesia as a country full of people wearing colorful "traditional" costumes but run by a small coterie of Javanese army officers. This view was perfectly captured in a project Suharto's wife, Ibu Tien Suharto, created in the 1970s: the Beautiful Indonesia-in-Miniature Theme Park, a kitschy combination of Disneyland and the Holland-in-miniature Madurodam. This melding of American and Dutch models was fitting for a regime enchanted by the wealth and glamour of California but firmly rooted in the authoritarian habits of the colonial state. From its inception, the New Order also showed a reckless disregard for the impact of its economic policies on the rural masses, an attitude that was dramatized in the construction of a large dam, the Kedung Ombo project, in the 1980s, when Central Javanese farmers displaced from their land tried to obtain fair compensation from the state. Like thousands of other Indonesians forced off their land, they were cheated by corrupt officials—and they were expected to give up quietly. A group of them, championed by Mangunwijaya among others, chose instead to fight and even enjoyed a provisional triumph when on appeal a court ordered that their compensation be increased. But the Supreme Court eventually overturned that verdict. The final portion of Chapter Six of *Durga/Umayi*, like much of Chapter Seven, epitomizes the enchantment with shiny surfaces, the globalizing pretensions, and the arrogance evident in the Beautiful Indonesia and Kedung Ombo projects, and a great many other projects like them, in Iin's grandiose multinational educational and historical theme park megaproject and its devastating and unforeseen impact on her brother.

By 1991, the year *Durga/Umayi* was published, the New Order was twenty-five years old and impervious to all challenge. Its principles were simple: economic expansion would proceed apace, but no power would be shared outside Jakarta's military and political elite. No political discussion of any import was permitted. Any hint of criticism brought immediate, heavy-handed repression, justified by reference to phantom traces of leftist elements. Civil service jobs and government services were available only to those able to prove they had "clean" backgrounds, that is, that not only they themselves but also their parents and other relatives were untainted by any politically compromising history. Periodic sham elections pleased the U.S. government and other foreign observers, but political parties were so closely monitored and manipulated as to be inert. Economic liberalization as promoted by the World Bank and IMF received intermittent support, but the Suharto family refused to give up its percentage cut in all major projects, and as Suharto's children and then grandchildren grew older their rapacity proved an increasingly heavy burden on all economic activity. People were left to look back nostalgically to a world they had lost, before there was such widespread wealth and before there was such rapid urbanization—and the attendant clogging of roads, airwaves, and the middle class's arteries that development had brought about.

It is in this condition of modernizing frenzy and social and political gridlock that the novel concludes. Much hangs in the balance for Iin at this point. But her choices are severely constrained, and we don't really know of any options available to her that would enable her to escape the disastrous implications all of her actions—she suddenly sees—would entail. The reappearance of her beloved Microphone, image of her direct connection to Indonesia's poor, represents a *deus ex machina,* the necessarily magical because otherwise unimaginable and impossible rescue of Indonesia's people from the consequences of their leaders' appalling moral indifference.

In an Afterword to this translation of the novel, I consider the novel relative to another important fictional rendering of Indonesian history, Pramoedya Ananta Toer's *Buru Quartet,* and I discuss Mangunwijaya's role in Indonesian public discourse. At this point, however, a reader should turn to the novel itself and start in on its brilliantly idiosyncratic but acutely insightful rendering of Indonesia's recent past.

In the original edition of the novel, the author put footnotes at the bottom of some pages, providing Indonesian readers with translations of foreign words (English, French, or Dutch), explanations of some now-forgotten acronyms, and other brief bits of information he felt they might need. This device gives the text, already grammatically complicated, a look of still greater complexity, as do the italicized foreign words that crop up in many places. The coupling of this academic apparatus with an often highly colloquial style makes the text incongruous in yet another way, an added incongruity Mangunwijaya probably savored. In order to maintain the look of the original text, I have chosen to include both the italicization of foreign words and phrases (including English ones) and the original footnotes in my translation, even though many readers will find them superfluous at times, and at other times inadequately detailed.

But since many readers of this translation will lack some knowledge that Mangunwijaya could assume in his Indonesian readers, I have appended further notes after the translation. These notes are not signaled in the text but rather keyed to pages and words or phrases. A reader who is puzzled or curious about historical, mythological, or other references in the text can turn to these notes for brief explanations. But readers who are made impatient by such interruptions of their reading can ignore these notes or turn to them at the end of a chapter, as they wish.

Every translation forces choices upon its fashioner. In the case of this novel, in which language play runs riot on every page, trying to remain true to both sound and sense presents particularly severe challenges. I have often had to choose between strict adherence to the sense of the original and loyalty to its author's delight in puns, rhymes, and other verbal high jinks. At the same time, I have made every effort to reproduce as faithfully as possible the extraordinary nature of Mangunwijaya's sentence structure, and even his punctuation. Indonesian, particularly as spoken by Javanese, often names some topic at the beginning of an utterance or set of utterances and then refers back to it without needing to name it again or even to mark its place with a pronoun. Mangunwijaya takes advantage of this device to pile phrase upon phrase with reference to some earlier topic, but often in a manner so extravagant that the specific referent becomes hard to fathom. The resultant ambiguity makes even a highly literate Indonesian reader sometimes lose track of what a sentence actually refers to. At the same time, Mangunwijaya will stretch a sentence out over many lines or even pages and then suddenly end with a surprising twist. English must be bent and stretched to accommodate some of these literary tactics. But I wish to assure the reader that the quirks in the translation, and the ebullient liberties taken in tone and syntax, represent conscious efforts to carry into English qualities very much present in the original.

# Acknowledgments

Aware of my interest in Javanese shadow plays, Cara Ella Bouwman first brought Mangunwijaya's *Durga/Umayi* to my attention when we happened to meet in Salatiga in 1994. I was immediately enthralled by the novel, and when she mentioned that she was translating it into Dutch, I began thinking about translating it into English. The prospect was daunting, however, and it was only with the encouragement of Father Mangunwijaya and several other friends that I eventually decided to pursue the project. When I attended Tony Day's and Keith Foulcher's conference, held at Sydney University in 1998, on how the insights of postcolonial studies might benefit scholars working in Indonesian literature, I realized how great a contribution the novel made both to Indonesian studies and to contemporary fiction. I was fortunate to receive grants from the National Endowment for the Humanities and the University of Texas at Austin for the academic year 1999–2000 to make the translation. Bishop I. Suharyo and Father J. Pujasumarta of Semarang, and Father Budi Susanto of Yogyakarta, graciously arranged copyright permission. Bapak Rasito helped me with many questions about the text, and Ariel Heryanto and Anom Kusumasari answered queries about fine points of translation. Keith Foulcher and Barbara Hatley provided invaluable critical readings of my introduction, notes, and afterword. Michael Duckworth of the University of Washington Press has been an enthusiastic and aggressive editor. Finally, Leslie Morris has supported the project from its inception and over the many years since. To all of these people I am very grateful.   W.K.

# Durga / Umayi

# Foreshadowplay

Whereupon once at that time
an idea a tale old stories betold about
ooh oahem ahem ohem ohem ohem my dear manly spouse
ooh oahem ahem ohem my pretty wife pretty one
my dear ohem oahem ahem,
they say it is told sighing sadly that whereupon
once at that time Goddess Durga
vaunting voracious vile-mouthed queen from
muddy murky Corpstenchfield, meaning
the Place of Banishment Smelling of Corpses,
actually once whereupon way back once yes once
a goddess attractive arresting imposing sweetly named
as sweet as the honey in Arjun's Honeyrealm: Uma or Umayi,
queen maharani of heaven in its glorious beauty,
dwelling place sublime abundant resplendent
of many gods and goddesses, divine lords and ladies,
yook yokem yokem yokem pleasure.
Thereupon it is told:
Noble Lord Brilliantjewel Maharaja of Heaven
whereupon once at one time
still far from approaching twilight, when
the season's rains had vanished

beyond the heavens, and the earth *ngarcapada**
fresh refreshed cleansed again without dust,
the sky clear cloudless beautiful boundless
crimson golden-gilt beclouded with gleaming borders
crocheted in whirling patterns leafy leafed
sandalwood coppered gold-leaf copper-red, thus Lord Guru
Noble Brilliantjewel Maharaja of Heaven
was seized of a great desire to take pleasure in travel
saaaay say I say sweet one pretty princess-devotee Yi
    Umayi,
let us take to the upper reaches
to lave our hearts to perfume our senses
so that eternal evivva come mount the gold chariot
drawn by horses with wings, crossing the bridge of the sky
the seven-hued rainbow come
saaaay say I say sweet one pretty princess-devotee Yi Umayi!
Thus oooh oahem ahem ohem ohem like egrets
sent circling smoothly surveying the rainbow they
    soared
with pleasure
two god-goddesses divine lord and lady the Pillar
of Heaven with his great sakti who was
attractive arresting imposing,
delighting in harmony playfully teasing, enchanted
    enthralled
in enjoyment and environs entrancing
without end.
Yet oooh oahem ahem ohem ohem manly spouse
and pretty woman my dear wife dear wife dear,
his softshell astraddle excited unchecked long with desire

---

(Middle World=earth. [All notes are by the author except material in
brackets, which is supplied by the translator.]

of the Noble Maharaja of Heaven unrestrained
slipped slithered slid up stuck out and strained
against noble Sakti Maharani who
lustrous luminous looking askance burst out
   laughing for
her lovely locks that made her so attractive
caressed by the wind mischievous pranksterish
wishing to tease to importune then once sundered softened

rolled her rocked her passionately, oooh
husband husband manly spouse
pleeease oh pleeease pretty one wife!
It was clear it was obvious it was evident ooh
husband wife,
such great lust passion spirits sprites could not
be answered assumed appreciated assuaged by
the noble goddess princess-devotee silk-mannered
sweet-tempered sterling-hearted goddess Umayi;

no way could divinities of glorious stature
of illustrious prestige go
rubbing rolling spreadeagling sprawling
shameless freely observed
by any common person by any living thing.
Thus oh no oh no all the more Lord Mahalingga
Lord Supermale rages rifles rouses
raps rasps, all the shriller sharply stingingly,
with rough rude words of contempt noble Sakti Umayi,
till exploding in curses swearwords oaths imprecations
stingray-catastrophe and oooh what's happening oooh
husband manly spouse pretty one wife oooh-o-oh horror
to make the hair stand on end, oh no oh no no no
who would not cry out:
Great Guru crazed confused with lust suddenly

bears a wild boar's fangs the result
of a taunt: acting like such a pig behaving like such
   a boar!
Thus the husband manly spouse pretty one wife,
fruit of the sakti's fury, because the goddess is
   great sakti
meaning
force of energy force of skill
force of readiness force of movement force of life
the lord god is her mate.

On the other hand oooh husband manly spouse
pretty one wife, Great Mahalingga Supermale
god minister of heaven Brilliantjewel
exacts his revenge and oh no no no
how could one's soul not be disturbed;
great goddess Uma attractive arresting imposing
changes to become a loutish female lump
like a louche lizard bitch with a body like a slab
clownish ulcerous foul-smelling giving fright

with an ogress's face the eyes of a sprite a flat stubby
   nose,
grinning mouth, cassava-like breasts
only one hand that can move,
Togog's fat buttocks and fungus-blotched legs;
and what's more oh no oh Wretched World oh
   Abominated Ass
who would not feel faint to hear
the stern sentence for Durga Corpstenchfield,
former Umayi gentle mannered but ill-fated
her mouth moldering muckering a leech for a tongue,
henceforth must cohabit with her own husband's
seed, that of Lord Guru who
crazed with cheap worthless lust improper

obscene, far from the demeanor of a true guru and sage,
to live in the manner of beasts to be frank
yes with Lord Kala, Master of Time
whose appearance is revolting repulsive,
devourer of living creatures and god of death death
death oooh Lord of Death mortolord, ladymorta
   malymordo
mortolatus tuslatomor, mortopanem nempatomor
laconus lacona, si domicus si domica
si sidanus si sidani, si regimagus spec imagus
si dometa
si dometus
andometa
modatane . . .

# Chapter One

Nyonya Nusamusbida, or properly: *Puan* Nusamusbida, according to a high-ranking authority of the Indonesian language who, from the time of *Gouverneur Generaal* Tjarda van Starkenborgh-Stachouwer[1] right on toward the year 2000 was a committed New Literatus, an advocate of the unifying language of Greater Pan Malay for the entire Southeast Asia Southern Region;[2] well it's true the term *puan* is far more authentic, more scholarly and psychologically more uplifting than the title *nyonya,* which is a common misusage among the heirs of the Balai Pustaka, even though it reeks like fish paste of a down-home Market Malay, thus is inappropriate to serve up at a banquet table or at an official podium at the national level; so maybe in the local spirit of compromise and of the harmony so much promoted by the authorities we'd do best to call the lady Pu(an) Nyo(nya) Nusamusbida, or in full *Punyo* Iin Sulinda Pertiwi Nusamusbida (even though the lady herself preferred to be called by her more familiar names Iin or Linda or Tiwi or later, Nus or Nussy or Bi, depending on the situation and mood); anyway this *punyo* was filthy rich, surpassing even that legendary personage Nyai Singo-

---

1. The last Governor General of the Dutch East Indies.
2. Sutan Takdir Alisjahbana.

barong from Pekalongan, made famous by the story, half-history, half-fiction, of the Maiden Mendut and her lover Pronocitro—and this has been acknowledged indeed documented in the computers of the Southeast Asian Business Data Center.

The only trouble is, just as an aside, the fighters of the younger generation who are joined together in the, you know, the Movement for Women's Rights (which old-fashioned male chauvinist pigs[3] often deride as the Moving Parts of Women's Rice) don't choose to recognize Miss Iin or Sister Linda or Auntie Wi or Comrade Tiwi or Nus or Madame Nussy or Sis Bi (depending on the situation and mood) as a *woman* let alone grant her the title *punyo,* but just as a female; but that of course comes from a normal if irritating trait, though one never yet susceptible of complete analysis by Charles Darwin or Sigmund Freud[4] or any local magic specialists or paranormals, namely, social and personal jealousy, a strange urge that refuses to appreciate how much our *punyo* Nusamusbida matters as an asset and source of national pride.

And anyway, what's so bad about calling someone a female when they say it brings out the meaning *a creature that has a womb and breasts* period (unlike the word lady: *the matron of the household who is venerated as a font of wisdom*) so actually it goes more toward the sexual side, because, well here we are back to the jealousy thing, you've got to admit that like it or not when it comes to nonmasculinity Sis Nus Madame Nussy (just feel how luscious that sound is, Nnuuss) clearly knows how to make her own way, but she really is something to long for, both financially and physically, in a word, she's a legend on both counts, the equal of Queen Ken Dedes who not only had the means to enchant the handsome but hapless Ken Arok, consumer of Empu Gandring's potent dagger, but also they say enchanted the Proclaimer of Indonesia's Independence, Bung

---

3.  Feminists' term of abuse for men: rude egotistical pigs.
4.  Launcher of the theory of evolution, and pioneer of psychoanalysis.

Karno of course; as long as we remember that he didn't experience Ken Dedes's charm as a statesman but rather as a human being, the extension of the organ of the millions of inhabitants of these tens of thousands of islands that coil about the equator like an emerald sash.

Perhaps *Madame* Nussy can be counted among what people from France, that country of *troubadour,*[5] call a *femme fatale,*[6] but we must always bear in mind that the Indonesian context differs completely from what experts from foreign countries, especially the West, make subject to analysis; clearly the meaning of Ken Dedes is different from Isolde of Old Germany, or Shakespeare's Lady Macbeth, very different too from Cleopatra of Egypt or Helen of Greece; still apart from all that, what can *fatale,* that is, the source of misfortune, mean for this Emerald Equator country which, it's true, surrendered and submitted out of exhaustion for such a long time to the Netherlands' tricolored flag, yet did once work up its courage to fling itself into the crater of the Great Revolution by means of a Proclamation wagered with rivers of blood and tears, as Bung Karno so often put it rhetorically but not boastfully in his speeches. No, Auntie Wi can't be faulted just because she works magic on people, because she's a career woman and stupefyingly sexy to boot, and please don't forget (it's too bad how few people know, or know but don't wish to acknowledge) that our *Punyo* Pertiwi Nusamusbida, even though she's filthy rich and for that reason powerful at the highest echelons, in her heart of hearts she still vouchsafes, like a pearl in its shell, a self-sacrificing, public-spirited and kindly soul, full of understanding and still in search of love; oh, it's a misunderstanding, clearly a misunderstanding that makes the tragedy of jealousy rise up without justification: people are just too quick to buy into base, primordial emotions and fights, with no compass and no rudder, just a plain gas pedal and no brakes, which is the main reason why the VOC's colonial policy of *divide et*

---

5. Wandering singers in ancient France.
6. A woman who brings misfortune.

*impera* succeeded in subjugating a country as big as this one for so long, and why parliamentary democracy didn't run smoothly here. But fortunately, our *punyo* is really exceptional, she's not sad or angry but rather pleased and proud to see the steadily increasing ranks of the envious, it's clear proof of how great and still growing her status and prestige are that she is the object of so much envy; well it's not unusual, really, because a lot of wives are happy and proud if their husbands are jealous (the reverse may not hold true), a reliable indicator that a wife's exchange rate is still high on the currency market. But of course for Auntie Wi Miss Bi the primary meaning of "the market" isn't a merely figurative one but rather literally the speculative market in currency and paper that is centered in the ritzy Capital City Independence Avenue district; in places like that Miss Bi really feels like a porpoise in the Moluccan Sea, her enchanting chest swells and her bliss peaks till strangely enough Miss Bi often feels like it's a shame, really a shame that little Iin was born a girl. Supposing she had slid out of the womb of her mother (the wife of a retired former corporal, hanger-on of the *garrison of the Second Division of the Royal Netherlands Indies Army*) who sold *gethuk-cothot*[7] that people were very fond of because the cassava she used was really tasty, grown in the special volcanic soil donated by Mt. Sumbing, anyway supposing Iin had been born with a secret amulet rod thingy like Rockefeller had, and Rothschild and also Ken Arok and every pedicab driver for that matter, then surely Sis Linda would long since have become another Oei Tiong Ham,[8] the Tiger Balm King, who back in the Dutch period once bought a big mansion in the heart of Beijing, or maybe like Khassoghi,[9] Mitsubishi,[10] or maybe even Onassis who got to stick his needle into the widow of the president of the world's most powerful nation.

---

7. Fried cassava filled with sugar syrup and shaped into little flat rounds.
8. A billionaire in Semarang in the Dutch Indies period.
9. A billionaire Arab weapons dealer.
10. Bankers in Japan whose wealth dates back centuries.

As a matter of fact Iin had often been irritated something terrific, unable to figure out how come her older brother *kembar-dampit*[11] (strange to say he's hit a dead end, happy to this day just to be a dim farmer living with his in-laws in the dry dusty desertous hills) could always go roaming around chasing after kites broken off from their strings on the main road or in the neighbors' yards, didn't get into trouble for stealing mangoes in the garden behind Haji Hammam's, and furthermore didn't have to do chores like washing the dishes, sweeping the floor or sewing torn pants like Iin had to, so the result naturally was that the little sister was jealous in the extreme because of this traditional discrimination; nevertheless, in the end, and especially once God had bestowed upon her femininity a pair of tomatoes full of seven spells to draw the crowds, Sis Linda congratulated herself ever more smugly upon her natural and inherited talent and the power women possessed over others, which she felt was basic to their nature (thus clearly due to the wishes of the All-Powerful God) and always made her puff up her chest; so she felt grateful that in her childhood and youth as a font of wisdom in the making she was discriminated against, taken down and toughened up by an old-style upbringing.

When Iin Linda was going off to middle school, her father, the ex-corporal in the KNIL (later *heiho*[12] and a sergeant major in the TKR then a lieutenant, then captain in the TNI appointed posthumously) provisioned her with a prettier, more meaningful name: Pertiwi; you see at the Sempoerna Elementary School graduation party, formerly it was the *Bijzondere H.I. School*[13] opposite the old colonial-era Regency Office on Pendowo Street, Magelang, Linda, big for her age, was chosen by her teacher (later to become a famous composer in

---

11. Twins, one male, one female.
12. A soldier helping out in the Japanese army during the Pacific War.
13. Dutch-medium Private Elementary School for children of ethnic Indonesians.

the capital who in the heroic, if economically hopeless, atmosphere
at the start of the Japanese period got a chance to fall in love with
this girl who was big for her age) to play the role of the symbolic
figure Mother Pertiwi, although it was just a nonspeaking part in what
used to be called a *tablo*[14] all she had to do was wear fancy clothes
and look sad and downcast in a grown-up way but with her head
held high full of nationalist self-regard, yearning for independence;
in fact ever since her soon to be a famous composer teacher had taken
a shine to her, Pertiwi young and green as she was began to appreciate what a pleasure it was to be a young woman with the power
to enchant or whatever it was she didn't know yet, on account of
the fact that a new notion was taking root, very different from the
feudal mind-set of "the flower waiting for the bee," a whole new
determination—aggressive, on the offensive, mounting the charge—
that arose together with the New Order of Greater East Asia Under
the Leadership of Our Older Kinsmen the Dai Nippon; a dangerous
attitude, one that an indigenous tongue might very well liken to a
*peri*, "a spirit in the form of a beautiful woman who makes men stupid and act crazed like a chicken getting slaughtered," and since men
almost always are stupid, it's pretty clear just how dangerous it would
be to let a young woman like Linda Tiwi take charge, all the more
so given that she's a street kid who nursed on dynamite and got pow-
dered with ammunition from the time she was a baby.

Her father, who sent her off with that beautiful name of Pertiwi, used to be a *soldaat*[15] in the Dutch Indies Royal Army, with the
right to decorate his shirtsleeves with the blood-red epaulets of a *kor-
poraal;* he was descended from a family originally from Bagelen, Kedu,
linked by tradition to the KNIL, with many ancestors loyal to the
Dutch Kingdom, who moreover fought actively and proudly against

---

14.  *Tableaux* (French) = picture. Diorama on stage with human "statues."
15.  Soldier.

the troops of Prince Diponegoro and Abas Sentot[16] and you can be sure never got left behind in the colonial wars in Bali and Aceh under the Dutch tri-colored flag. It was a good thing the Japanese came in and drove the Dutch out so that Young Man Obrus (the Javanese version of *overste,* alias lieutenant colonel), our corporal in the KNIL, could turn his rudder right around and become a *heiho* who spent the largest part of his service time in Halmahera, at that time the biggest depot for the Japanese navy, which was responsible for controlling the South Pacific. A good thing too that in June 1945, on the very day that Bung Karno first formulated the Pancasila in the *Dokoritsu Zyunbi Tyoo Sakai,* our *heiho* Obrus was sent to Java, sailing together with a platoon of Korean soldiers under the command of a *Kenpetai*[17] lieutenant to safeguard five tons of Dutch silver coins on their way from Halmahera to Surabaya; now thanks to God's munificence their ship was attacked by Allied pursuers and in the end the five tons of silver coins sank along with the Korean soldiers and the *Kenpetai* lieutenant carrying all those heavy weapons, so that *heiho* Obrus alone of all those people was safe (due of course to the prayers of his mother in Kebumen), even though he drifted for three days on the Java Sea, landing on the coast at Lasem; weak but still alive; this was called a good thing a moment ago because they say that *heiho* who knew too many Japanese secrets were always killed; so in this way Obrus was safe, rescued by a fisherman, but because he was afraid to go back to the Japanese army on the chance they might accuse him of sinking those five tons of Dutch coins and killing so many soldiers from Nippon, with the intention in the future of sneakily fishing that wealth back up from the bottom of the sea, so our *heiho* decided to desert and steal into Yogya, not Kebumen because the *Kenpetai* would look for him there, and it turned out quite

---

16. Top commander of Prince Diponegoro's army.
17. The Japanese Army Military Police.

by accident—but fortunately so—that he got caught up in a group of anti-Japanese heroes near the ice factory in Pathuk.[18]

There it was that the ex-corporal in the KNIL ex-Japanese *heiho* became an independence fighter in the heart of the future capital city of the Republic of Indonesia while occasionally going to Kebumen, but great was his disappointment that he could only find his twin Iin, orphaned a year already and being cared for by their grandparents, because their mother in a short time, just two days, had died, cut down by the plague that sometimes raged for a while in various regions during the colonial period when everything was scarce; it was a shame really because their mother (whose name was Legimah because she was born on a Friday Legi) had only spent two nights, as a good niece, visiting her uncle whose village, unbeknownst unfortunately to all, was at the time being attacked—but as fate would have it, no one knew this—by that vicious epidemic, and she caught it and died in a frightful way; it truly was a shame because at that point Legimah was living a very comfortable and secure life as both a household servant and a mistress of a Japanese officer at the barracks, without of course the permission or for that matter the knowledge of her husband who was way off there in Halmahera. The villagers looked upon the unlucky death of the *heiho*'s wife as the judgment of an All-Just God (and a judgment on that Japanese officer who of course got moved and quarantined), but the ex-*heiho* Obrus himself, who in the end of course did indeed find out about the secret relations between his wife and the samurai in the barracks, considered his wife's passing—the wife whom he very much loved—the benevolent act of a true Javanese wife who was willing to sacrifice all as a means to assure the well-being of her husband and twin children; as a matter of fact as a former *heiho* who rec-

---

18. An underground group of fighters in the Japanese period who led the way in seizing power from the Japanese in Yogya.

ognized he was only of low rank but knew about the world of soldiers in wartime, Obrus, the guy from Kedu, admitted frankly in his heart (of course it couldn't be said straight out) that he was even a little proud that it was none other than his wife who was specially chosen by an officer from the Nation of the Older Kinsmen, who however bad they might be still did perform the great service of chasing the Dutch out of Indonesia; convinced as he was that in any case God was All Merciful and All Forgiving, and furthermore: why should Legimah get put down and condemned for having been the respected mistress for a while of a respected samurai, when here he was, a dumb *heiho,* delivered safely from the waves of the Java Sea and the air raids of the Allies who bombed Halmahera every single day, and when to tell the truth he himself had fallen in with the customs and rhythms of the dumb Japanese soldiers who slept with prostitutes every other day, prostitutes made available by the dumbest of them all, the logistical staff of the Dai Nippon army at the depot? No, Obrus, Kebumen's son, guileless and good and as instinctively fair as a child, was not going to curse Legimah just because she made her living by sleeping, clean and neat, in the beautiful room that had once been occupied by the godly Dutch overlords who, justice served, then got their turn to be coolies in Burma or some other place to be sacrificial victims and rinse away a little of their sins for having colonized the homeland for so many centuries. It's a sure thing that Legimah's death by the nondiscriminatory plague had a positive sense and outcome, at the very least, according to the reckoning of this rent-a-*heiho,* that his wife, before becoming a helpful go-between between heaven and her husband and children, had surely turned into some kind of sacrificial victim for them, once she had repaid the three and a half years (exactly the same length of time as the Japanese occupation) she was sentenced to in the emergency hell of war in the world hereafter; because the fact was that our Obrus always escaped unscathed from every mortal danger in battle or revolution, and meanwhile one of those twin children of theirs managed to grow up to be a farmer, okay so not a rich one, just a plain farmer but able to stand on his own two feet, honest, and well-regarded; in contrast to his twin sister who managed to become a fantastic career woman, beautiful, intelligent, and able to sate herself on all of life's pleasures; so see it all balanced out in the end, and Obrus's life was a fruitful one after all.

Thus at that point in time this beloved father, ex-corporal, ex-*heiho,* and retired lieutenant, peacefully awaited the moment of his life's end in his villa in Embong Menur Bayeman Magelang, a luxurious quarter like Menteng in Jakarta, only mini, where in the past only high-status Dutch bigwigs and their kids could live, but where he could stay now thanks to his daughter Sulinda's money. Obrus was always convinced that his death would be caused not by disease or accident but rather because he had reached the end of his allotted time and had completed his duties as a man of the barracks whose responsibility it was to defend the independence and sovereignty of the Republic of Indonesia, whose Proclamation of Independence on August 17, 1945, was acknowledged by the whole world; thus at this time he sensed once again how deeply he longed for Legimah, who long ago before they were married had willingly let him rape her, barracks style, among the clumps of yellow flowers and purple bougainvillea on the slopes next to the Plengkung canal that was always dark after the sun went down, even though the main road, always busy, with electric streetlights, was only ten meters down from it; ah, Retired Lieutenant Obrus was indeed filled with longing for his first love Legimah who was born on Friday Legi back when the colonial era in Magelang still felt pleasant and safe and tranquil, and prosperous, too, for the likes of a KNIL soldier with red epaulets, at least in those days there was nothing to make people all worried or anxious about what might happen, like the price of rice and other staples going up, or their children's SPP[19] and such; yes at this time

---

19.  Sumbangan Pembinaan Pendidikan [Contributions for Educational Development, i.e., school fees].

our Obrus guileless and good native son of Kebumen Bagelen was convinced that he would get to meet up once again with Legimah who would certainly already have been forgiven by God the All Merciful and All Forgiving since clearly she had long since served out her sentence of three years; yes well it stands to reason, if even a Japanese officer, who was crude and what's more irresponsible even if possessed of a long sword, if he chose Legimah to be his mistress, then surely God who is All Beneficent and certainly not cruel and very responsible, now surely God would long since have shown his indulgence to Legimah given that out of loyalty to her husband and children she had willingly become the sacrificial means via the plague epidemic to assure the well-being of her husband and children; and here that old *heiho* Obrus (and God had certainly noticed this) had gone off the deep end, imitating the Japanese soldiers fooling around with women practically every day, and here it was Legimah who had to pay the consequences, oh God, forgive this beast Obrus who accepts without question getting cast into a hell worse still than Halmahera when it was being attacked every day by the Allied air force, as long as it's just three and a half years, exactly as long as our homeland was occupied by the Dai Nippon army; but please Lord then let Obrus be happy together with Legimah who surely in the hereafter is a thousand times more beautiful, just like the nymphs in those Indian films, well all right if everything's got to be like it was in the KNIL era, that's okay with old Obrus, too, because that was a time when things were pleasant and peaceful and full of pleasure for our KNIL corporal Obrus, only it would be good if it were a KNIL era under the Red and White Indonesian flag. Certainly God can make the hereafter like that because God is All Powerful, even though it has to be admitted that it couldn't happen in this world, but dear Lord God, isn't the world hereafter completely different from this one?

So it was that at exactly 10 o'clock on the morning of the Seventeenth of August, when all of Indonesia was observing a moment of silence while listening to the sacred text of the Proclamation of Independence, he passed away, Retired Lieutenant Obrus from Kebumen Bagelen Kedu who was always faithful to Wilhelmina, Queen of the Kingdom of the Netherlands, very faithful to Tenno Heika in Tokyo to whom every morning he showed respect bowing very deeply, almost to the ground, and of course 100 percent faithful to the Republic of Indonesia which he loved second only to Legimah, yes he passed away, quietly, peacefully, proudly, secure in his beliefs and set to go, as is appropriate to a human being of good faith who is agreeable to both God and his fellows, even if his sins sometimes weighed more than five tons. The burial was very touching with trumpet and drums moving people deeply, as airs in praise of heroes brought tears to the eyes of fading patriots with their wire tendons and iron bones and machine-gun mouths, and an eighteen-gun salute rent the sky, one hour before the carnival parade of the Eighteenth of August passed along the major arteries, and the ceremony was even attended by none other than the Division Commander himself because Sergeant Major Obrus had once served as his adjutant when they were guerrillas together in the region of Mt. Sumbing and Sindoro as the special officer in charge of the important task of attending to his food and laundry; although admittedly without the flashy *glamour* seen in patriotic films and made-for-TV movies that are often shown to stir the nationalist fires of the younger generation, still at the time the assistance of the sort provided by Brother Obrus was truly vital to the outcome of the guerrilla tactics of this commander, who, so touchingly, never forgot the services his adjutant had rendered and moreover was good enough to attend the burial service of the worthy Retired Captain Obrus; yes Obrus the model adjutant who in the guerrilla days often felt ashamed and at fault for daring to force himself like a parasite on the poor villagers in the hinterland, but what can you do but forgive and forget, in the old days there was no logistical budget underwritten by the careful calculations of the National Planning Development Board and the blessings of the National People's Representative Council of the Republic of Indonesia and so forth, so that all food and any other needs had to come from the people, via the village headman; see now war really is war, it's not politics with people in ties and cocktail glasses in their hands wrangling among departments about who gets what.

For *Punyo* Pertiwi the passing of her father gave rise to feelings of sadness mixed with anger because at his death he only got a posthumous promotion to the rank of captain, when in actual fact if you considered his service it should have been lieutenant colonel at the very least, in line with his name, Obrus, which once again don't forget means *overste* or lieutenant colonel. Obviously this tragedy only happened because at the time Sis Tiwi was fending off the indecent approaches of the officer who was in charge of the whole matter of promotions; it wasn't because the officer was ugly or sadistic or anything, oh as for that he was a regular Gatotkaca, rather it was just because—well, it's silly: the good man suffered from high blood pressure and for that reason always ate a fistful of garlic every morning and man did that ever have an effect on the quality of his circulatory respiration. Supposing he had just been willing to substitute something else for the garlic, like menthol mints or lozenges, then no doubt Sis Tiwi would not have driven too hard a bargain even if the gentleman did have a wife and four children, what the heck, the important thing was for her beloved father Obrus to be buried with the insignia of two stars on a black ground edged in gold; it's a historical tragedy almost beyond belief and yet it really happened, a hero's stature got decided just by the smell of garlic.

Her encounter with her twin older brother on this occasion of paying their last respects to their dear father was very warm on the part of the younger sister, without bothering about the lowly status of this mountain farmer whose character and attitude were really strange, the exact opposite it seemed from *Punyo* Morningstar of the Capital, as a matter of fact this brother from the boonies was startled out of his skin when suddenly without the slightest warning or preparation he was getting hugged and kissed in front of everyone by his very own younger sister who was only seventeen minutes younger than he was; kissing him in the metropolitan international Hollywood style which made him ashamed and confused in front of the assembled company of mourners, all the more so since it turned out that a little bit of her lipstick got left on his cheek; boy is it ever a pain having a sister like Iin Linda Tiwi who's a star in the business world and acts like she's in an ad all the time, but oh well, what can you do, you can't fight the way your fate turns out even if it's the fate of not being rich, just a boondock farmer living at his in-laws'. It's a good thing his wife wasn't mad and jealous because wasn't this metropolitan *punyo* his very own sister, a twin but with a different fate? Of course once she got home to the hills his wife got razzed a lot by her relatives, asking why she didn't take on the metropolitan style as demonstrated by the well-heeled ladies of the Civil Servants' Ladies' Auxiliary association often appearing on the subdistrict office's television screen? Which of course causes genuine irritation among the wives who are not just wives at home but prime ministers like Margaret Thatcher and Benazir Bhutto, since they feel like they stand accused of being uncivilized, hicks still in need of getting accelerated-modernated, with consequences that often show up in food that "just happened" to get scorched or rice that smells smoky or clothes that "quite by accident" haven't gotten washed in a month's time, and so on, a timeless form of guerrilla warfare and one hard to do anything about. But in any case, Brojol, that was the name of *Punyo* Pertiwi's twin brother, always got not insignificant sums of money as gifts from the younger sister whom he used to kick when they were little because she wouldn't fix the buttons on his clothes when they came off; it was true, when it came to being good-hearted Iin was really above reproach even though she made her brother feel ashamed and inferior. His wife meanwhile only made him feel worse with all her ridicule: how come his sister was such a looker, stacked like a Eurasian, with well-proportioned hips, waist and those perfect breasts, all combined with that American face

(everything fabulous is American) whereas her honored husband had
Pétruk's looks and a body shaped like the fried cassava snacks his
dear departed mother used to sell as she squatted at the corner of
the Chinese temple near the town square; oh, now please forgive
her, Prime Minister Margaret Benazir, sister-in-law to Linda, if these
frank remarks are likely to upset people who don't know her, but
for Brother Brojol (he never spruced up his name in the Spanish fashion or the American or whatever else at the express wish of his wife),
as far as he was concerned it was precisely this kind of behavior that
guaranteed the intimate ties between them, affording them so much
happiness on the fertile black earth, a gift of the mountain named
Sindoro, meaning Lovely, where he was able to labor in the fields
of his mother's ancestors. Even among his friends the striking difference between the twin brother and sister often gave rise to questions that couldn't possibly be taken amiss because both the brother
and sister possessed exactly the same nose, Pétruk's nose according
to Brojol's wife, but actually it could be easily explained just with
Mendel's Law, bearing in mind that one of Ma Legimah's forefathers
was of Arab descent, and had Arab features that you still often saw
in those days in Magelang's Chinatown, amazingly tall with a head
covering called a *fez* or a cap like a court official's or a prince's in the
palace, only plain and what was really unusual, bright red like a hot
pepper, sporting a pigtail like a professor's, an open jacket and a white
shirt that was usually old and worn out, a checked sarong reaching
down to his calf and secured in the Malay style with a wide leather
belt, a wallet, and his feet in leather slippers that dragged as he walked,
making a rhythmic sound *dragdrag-clop-dragdrag-clop;* his face was
dark and shiny like polished shoes and he had just turned up from
the hot expanses of sandy Egypt, with a very distinctive nose like a
cockatoo's, and a pair of jet-black eyes; so both Brojol and Iin had
the same nose and the same eyes, too, that special jet black that you
can't order at the store but then again, in a more moderate, local version, not so extreme, so very becoming and cause for envy among

their friends who usually have flat noses and eyes that are sort of
Chinese and sort of Malay, what people used to call *yangko-yangko*.
Thus it was that scurrilous suggestions, along the lines of the brother
and sister being from the same womb but by two different fathers,
never got mooted or hooted in all their puzzled friends' many ruminations; such that in the end the one explanation that made any sense,
and as a matter of fact Obrus himself once said it when he was still
alive, was that in reality Brojol was descended from Lord Basuki, the
Snake King who lives beneath the ground, while Iin was descended
from Lord Wisnu whose palace is in heaven and uses the Garuda
Jetayu[20] as his Boeing jet. Both of those gods, according to his ancestors, were incarnated in the person of Corporal Obrus, who deposited
their seed in the womb of Goddess Dewani, aka Legimah, who, simple seller of fried cassava snacks near the Chinese temple at the corner of the town square though she was, nevertheless could clearly
be seen in her beauty to actually be a goddess; yes, well it's true that
then what needed to be explained was why Lord Wisnu would
choose to be incarnated in the body of a woman, namely, Iin's, something that has never been known to happen in all the palm-leaf man-
uscripts and all the shadow play stories, but Corporal Obrus just
palmed off an explanation, reflecting a fanatical regional pride, saying that the area of Kedu is an exceptional one, with its own wayang
stories, it doesn't always just trail along after Yogya-Solo, but rather
according to the History Chronicle, even the most powerful kings
of Mataram, like Sultan Agung, never dared to impose themselves
on the tax-exempt villages of Kedu to call up troops if they needed
them because they were wanting to mount expeditions against other
areas, as Mataram often demanded of such areas as Madiun, for example, and Pati, Lasem, Sumedang and so forth, so that's the way it was,

---

20. The garuda [mythical bird] that defended Goddess Sinta when she
    was kidnapped by Rahwana [in the Indian epic *Ramayana*].

even though Kedu did always help, voluntarily, the dynasty of Ki Ageng Pemanahan from Mataram it was clear proof of just how free the tax-exempt areas of Kedu were in the old days, and indeed still are down to the present day, due to the generosity of the venerable founding fathers of Merapi Merbabu Telomoyo Sumbing Sindoro and the courtiers of the Menoreh Mountains which are so full of chronicles both historical and ahistorical, and the temples of Borobudur-Mendut-Pawon as the most valuable heirlooms, ones uniquely able to spread the fame of the region of Kedu.

Thus it was that in good faith and not without mystical convictions Pa Brojol the incarnation of Lord Basuki willingly, indeed cheerfully, turned the soil as a farmer following after his fried-cassava-snack mother's side of the family, because in Brojol's view the important thing was his wife, his own Goddess Sri, who truly was a woman, aka a venerable font of wisdom, as has recently been theorized by the Movement for Women's Rights but had long since been put into practice in the daily lives of the Brojol husband-and-wife team, growers of coffee, tobacco, and of course rice (Javanese varieties, not the short ones lately given out by Government) in Karanggedong Candiroto Parakan; with the footnote that the fate of this descendant of the Lord King of Snakes by name of Basuki is no stain on anyone's reputation because for any farmer a snake and especially a python truly is the incarnation of Goddess Sri, distributor of fertility and prosperity; and that's no exaggeration because the farmer's greatest enemy is the rats that there are so many of recently that they're getting urbanized, moving to the cities, especially Jakarta; so the snakes that eat rats are clearly the fruit of God's mercy, and of inestimable value; as opposed to what city people think, always wanting to kill snakes, and what comes of it? Rats spread like wildfire and often these modern rats turn into people, now that's the disaster that comes of forgetting about Goddess Sri, who's like Goddess Pertiwi, partner in power to Lord Wisnu, or so thought Pa Brojol.

Unlike, completely unlike her twin brother who was content with his farmer's life in the boonies, Nyonya Pertiwi Nusamusbida (in actuality: Puan or, as a compromise: *Punyo* Pertiwi Nusamusbida) could only feel happy and content in a treacherous storm, in the midst of the roaring din of diesel engines and linked trucks that fart dark polluting exhaust fragrant with oil and go zigzagging, now in the middle lane now in the right lane then all of a sudden making a sharp left turn right turn, like the motorized trishaws flitting frenziedly about in traffic without giving a damn about hey there's a Mercedes or hey there's a city bus or a pedicab or a crazy pedestrian crossing the street calmly smoking a cigarette, hands in his pockets looking up to watch a couple of lovey mourning doves as though he were on the path through Pameungpeuk village, now to be in this world full of challenges strokes and scrapes that was paradise for *Punyo* Pertiwi alias Iin alias Linda alias Tiwi alias Nusi Musimus or Bi, depending on the situation and mood, dynamic, aggressive, on the offensive, attacking and sacking, falling and flailing, kicking 'em in the kneecaps, full of lustful excitement; sure, go right ahead and call her Mrs. Good Times, better that than Miss Feeblefatigue, what are those streamlined legs for that make her the equal of any model on the *catwalk,* uh *tigerwalk* if Iin's on it, since it's things as fierce as tigers that turn Auntie Wi Madame Nussy Miss Bi on, with that figure of hers impressively tall and attractive that makes you quiver, with an ass that begs to get kicked with Matheus Gullit Maradonna's soccer shoe to make it stop swaying, with her waist that always looks like it's playing with a hula hoop, Hawaii style, with that pair of festival carnival floodlights on her chest that just keep on swaying, restlessly, threateningly, explosively, crying out desire freedom *glasnost perestroika* but enclosed in coconut shells in accordance with Department of Religion and Bakorstanasda[21] regulations, with her head's aureole of shiny asphalt-black hair, a face italiano, classically Greek but with an Arab-Israeli reconciliation nose,

---

21.  Badan Hankam [Defense and Security Body] the replacement for Kopkamtib [Command for the Restoration of Security and Public Order].

a pair of gleaming eyes full of provocation and irresistible appeals, lips that with or without filter cigarettes between them have Maiden Mendut's stupefying power, power that gives the likes of Tumenggung Wiroguno (nowadays there are a great many wirogunos, since Bung Karno was laid to rest in Cipanas and Blitar) nervous fits and they're obliged to request hormone Y injections at paranormals' clinics so they won't fall too deeply into corruption and other irregularities just so that they can become unholy cigarettes for Mendut, the cigarette girl from Kedu; with the result that even families that have celebrated their golden wedding anniversary and have lots of grandchildren fall apart.

Nothing less than sensational was the appearance, but then, too, the achievements of this female (not a woman according to the views of the Leadership Council of the Movement for Women's Rights headquartered on college campuses) this one female who according to the neighbors who know her genealogy is the child of a former KNIL corporal and a fried-cassava-snack seller near the Chinese temple, but who according to *Who's Who,* the capital's influential publication, which is underwritten by several *bona fide* banks that have gone public, is the daughter of Professor Gilbert Washington Bsc. MBA PhD. ThD (not his real name) and Bendoro Raden Ayu Theresia Ursula Nurhayati Tejakusumaningrum (also not her real name), so two versions circulated, the villagers' version and the elite's version, but if you looked into it carefully it would become clear how Iin Sulinda Pertiwi's biography was always shrouded in a cloud of mystery, inviting a lot of impassioned guessing, and for just that reason served as a kind of advertising beacon making Auntie Tiwi or more properly Mrs. Perti all the more popular; among other things these endless puzzles became the sport of journalists; is the lady a widow or does she still live with a husband and if so who, because a woman as beautiful and as capable as Miss Bi would for sure once have had or might still have a husband, *nota bene*[22] a high-status one, most fittingly with

---

22. Note carefully!

a two-letter title Mr., *Meester in de Rechten,* or Dr., obtained from the University of Leiden, because this mysterious maiden from the Progo and Elo Valleys has a really extraordinary command of Dutch, even though she's only a product of the *Bijzondere H.I. School* on Pendowo Street opposite the old Regency Office of Magelang; but few people realize that this was the fruit of the girl Iin's own personal initiative, the girl who was jealous of her twin brother and wondered why he could always go out playing and roam around chasing after broken kites and come home with his clothes all dirty but didn't have to wash them whereas she had to be sweet and obedient, staying at home doing the dishes and helping Mother cook and so forth; and for that reason Iin tried to take revenge by going out roaming on her own but very cleverly visiting the home of the *Bijzondere H.I. School* principal, *Mijnheer* Van Gelder, on Kartini Street, who had two nice girls the same age as Iin, only they studied at the more prestigious *Europese Lagere School,*[23] so now it was from those two blonde Dutch girls that this daughter of the fried-cassava-snack seller from near the Chinese temple at the corner of the town square, who never felt inferior to or intimidated by anyone, obtained an *Algemeen Beschaafd Nederlandsch*[24] accent that really smacked of *boter met kaas* (butter and cheese), very different from those Eurasian kids from Pandestiran or the barracks bastards who do indeed speak Dutch but a Dutch always smacking of cassava. Once *Mijnheer* Van Gelder asked Iin, *"Wel wel mijn beste kind, wat wil je later worden?"* ("So my best child, what do you want to be when you grow up?") Instantly completely self-assured Iin replied, *"Koningin van het Nederlandsche Rijk"* ("Queen of the Kingdom of the Netherlands").

Back when her father came home without his *heiho* uniform to

---

23. Primary School for Dutch children.
24. The officially recognized Standard Polite Dutch.

look for her mother in Kebumen, Iin was in Jakarta, the official reason was because her aunt had invited her to look for work in Jakarta,
since there was no more money for her to keep up her schooling
once Ma Legimah passed away, but actually because this young
woman had a great desire to go to the capital just to see the
renowned Bung Karno; it wasn't as though Iin had suddenly become
a nationalist or become aware of what was called her people's struggle for freedom or anything like that; rather it was because this young
woman was fascinated by the speeches, full of fire and sledgehammers, of the much-respected engineer who was so good at firing up
people's courage, especially after they'd shown a long movie for free
to the general public on Magelang's town square telling the heroic
story of a Japanese tank commando named Nishizumi (not that it
appealed so much to the young woman); what happened on that
occasion is that Linda's heart first began to yearn uncontrollably to
meet with Bung Karno in person, she was that stupefied by the short
they showed before the film, brief and not scary but romantic, about
the song *Yaeshio* which was probably about beautiful Japanese
flowers or something, and who was the narrator for this romantic
song? None other than *the great Soekarno himself,* a young Bung Karno,
in a high, somewhat unsteady black velvet cap, a neat jacket and a
black tie with white polka dots or dark blue or dark red who knows
since the film was in black and white, but man oh man oh man what
about that pair of wide-set eyes in that handsome face, gleaming with
rays that could work magic on crowds; so when a youthful Bung
Karno's face appeared on the screen 6 × 4 meters in size, the whole
crowd in the square, maybe as many as a hundred thousand, all
together thundered like a storm, rumbling roaring cheering clapping
whistling—in a word, they had been put under a spell, electrified by
Soekarno's soul, even though all Bung Karno was doing in this short
film was praising the melodious and affecting song *Yaeshio,* not push-
ing political points, not treating tendentious topics that would lead

to demands for independence or anything else, just letting people hear his voice, sweet swaying swelling persuasive; Iin Sulinda forgot everything else about it, what she never forgot was just the handsome young man's face and a pair of eyes whose gleam cast an irresistible spell, for at the time Iin was a newly desirous newly ripening tropicana girl, comely lovely lustrous luscious, the fertile fruit of the Progo and Elo Valleys.

# Chapter Two

Her aunt had made her living since the time of the *Gouverneur-Generaal*s doing the washing and ironing for a Dutch family in East Pegangsaan Street; and when the Dutch professor's house where she offered her services was empty because Japan's Red Bull's-eye flag had replaced the Dutch Red, White and Blue one and then it got new occupants, a strapping big engineer, charismatic and really friendly and simpatico, from Bengkulu, taken there by a group of his admirers, it was dear Auntie who was asked by a go-between—and she accepted gladly—to take on the task that she had been doing for dozens of years already, washing and ironing the clothes of the elite neatly and precisely in the Hollanders' way for her new master and mistress, who were moreover very friendly to their servants. The master had lots and lots of friends and companions and acquaintances old and young, and over and over you could hear his voice, sweet swaying swelling but also thundering rumbling booming looming over radios which at that time you had to have a permit for, and everybody obviously knew his name, Soekarno. And since all those clothes she soaked washed wrung out bleached starched sprinkled ironed and folded neatly weren't just those of the great speechmaker engineer and his wife who was fair and caring and smooth and sweet and pretty and pleasant and pious and plucked from Bengkulu, but those of their friends companions buddies kin who were of course very numerous, with the permission of the lady of the house who was friendly and fair and smooth and sweet and pretty and pious, Iin Sulinda who now preferred to be called Tiwi joined her aunt, helping her clean everything dirty from among the most intimate possessions of the engineer master of the house who, quite accidentally it was a big *surprise* and quite startling, turned out to be her god and idol from that moving picture *Yaeshio* along with his young wife.

But not too long after that the status of *numero uno* god and idol went to a new idol, a young man with double pockets on his shirt and scouts' style green *shorts,* carrying a wooden rifle, with a black velvet cap at a jaunty angle on his bald head who looked fierce, he was originally from Randusari, Semarang, but was living at the barracks of Seinendan[1] or something like that anyway, who seemed to have the job of transporting secret letters, important ones, from the youth groups to Bung Karno; whose spirit soared talking about how great the Dai Nippon were and then the grandeur-of-Glorious-Indonesia, with his astonishing accounts of Free-Indonesia-Right-Now which Tiwi liked to listen to when this young man with the wooden gun sat on the veranda while enjoying tea and cookies Tiwi always got to serve him, always because the ladies working in the kitchen knew that Tiwi was very sweet on the bald youth with the velvet cap who was handsome and blazing with enthusiasm; let the girl from the Kedu hinterlands learn a little about the noble world of the political class who were bringing the masses to the boil to prepare them for Free Indonesia in the Future Days in the New Order of the East Asia Co-Prosperity Sphere Under the Leadership of Our Older Kinsmen the Dai Nippon, although not long after it turned out the young fresh-hearted hero didn't like terms he called covertly colonialist like freedom-in-the-future-days let alone New Order which he said was the same as the Old Order with all kinds of Greater East

---

1.  Young men's group with a military cast.

Asia controls and all that crap: under-the-leadership-of-our-older-kinsmen-the-Dai-Nippon and so on, man these dwarves with legs like O's as round as a mosque's drum are so arrogant, he said; Indonesia a gift from Japan wasn't what he and his comrades wanted, but 100% free Indonesia, seized by means of bloody revolution, full of youthful heroism worthy of the concept of Glorious Indonesia; such that Tiwi was deeply intoxicated not in the first place by his ideals but rather by his face which unfortunately was bald at the top but was still attractive covered with an elegant, romantic black velvet cap, and by the way that he spoke nodding and cocking his head, his thin pencil-line lips moving mouthing energetic pouting, that covered a tidy row of teeth all except for one that stuck a bit out of line, on the model of a male wild pig all fighting and feisty which Bung Karno had, too, and which just drove to distraction the heart of this girl who was in the thick of youthful yearning and tropicana ripeness, and on top of that had grown up in the rich black soil full of hopes of the Progo and Elo Valleys.

Thus great was Tiwi's astonishment when one fine morning in the month of August she listened to the shouts sobs anxious sighs of people in the kitchen who were worrying about the fate of Bung Karno and Ibu Fatmawati who was still nursing their baby—they'd been kidnapped the night before! from the house on East Pegangsaan Street which for some strange reason wasn't under guard or maybe it had been left unguarded accidentally on purpose; and then, all the more disturbing, according to one of the maids, the young man Tiwi was so taken with was in on this weird kidnapping of their own big, good-hearted leader;[2] just what is it that these stupid kids want, can they run things themselves as well as Bung Karno does? What's more according to rumors from Diponegoro Street Bung Hatta got kid-

---

2. The incident of Bung Karno and Bung Hatta's kidnapping to Rengasdengklok.

napped too, what *do* they want, things are already tough, prices are high there's shortages of everything, now we've got snot-nosed kids making everything tougher; there are swarms of beggars wandering around here in Jakarta and it's hard to find good rice, seems like things were better in the Dutch days but of course that was a damnable time never to be allowed to return and what does Japan actually want, those slit-eyed people like Chinese but they always smell of their soybean paste, really, when will life calm down without this war that goes on and on; is it going to turn out that Joyoboyo was right, that the Nippon people will only be in control for as long as a corn plant lives, since didn't Bung Karno and Bung Hatta just fly off some-place, Singapore was it or Saigon? are those different places? to be told that in a little while Indonesia can be free and the Red and White Indonesian flag can be flown freely, we can sing our anthem "Glo-rious Indonesia" as much as we please, everything's going to be fine provided everybody obeys the leadership of Bung Karno and Bung Hatta, but now along come these kids born yesterday carry-ing nothing more than rifles made out of wood and wearing vel-vet caps that are already getting threadbare jumping in to, well, to do what exactly? not a single person in the kitchen or at the well had a clue, hey not only them, not even the Japanese guys in charge did and neither it came out later did the Indonesian bigwigs and they were all stunned, oh God, so what does this mean can Indonesia ever really be free?

But in the days following Praise the Lord those wild kids brought back Bung Karno, Bung Hatta, Bu Fat, and above all and most impor-tantly little baby Guntur the poor thing who cried because his mother forgot to take along a bottle of milk for him, now about important things like this those youths certainly don't know the first thing; what do you expect? all guys know about is playing with sticks, those blunt sticks of theirs that know nothing about taking responsibility for the consequences, and don't understand that sometimes a milk bottle really matters, you can't just rely on a mother's breasts, especially the breasts of high-status people whose number one responsibility after all isn't to nurse a baby but to lead a nation; truly that guy Tiwi's always going on about has to get some sense beaten into him, sure he's scary and tough but what does he know about cute little humans that cry begging to be nursed, but all right, what's past is past, what matters is everyone's safe and back home again, because all that was the result of a misunderstanding as happens a lot between young people and their elders, after all, all of us were young once, right? and stubborn, and impatient and impetuous and incapable of ripe reflection; so that's that, the important thing, according to the rumors, tonight there's an extremely important meeting and maybe the next day Indonesia will already be free; so what needs to be done now is to arrange that tomorrow there be enough tea and sugar and some snacks to serve guests, and look here, who's going to make sure the floor gets swept and mopped, there are going to be a lot of guests tomorrow, and it's very important that the bathrooms and the WCs get cleaned and washed down with carbolic acid because man, in this Japanese era even the pee has gone Japanese, smelling more and more of soybean paste with a stinging Greater East Asia stench to it; you've got to be especially sure to keep young guys from wandering into the WC that's reserved for the use of Bung Karno and Bu Fatmawati; don't worry though about Bung Hatta, he's always very neat and precise, he's not only certain to come exactly 5 minutes before a meeting starts, he also pees exactly 5 minutes before getting into the car before a meeting or other official duties; unlike Bung Karno who sorry about this but sometimes he still pees by the fence at the side of the house or in the bushes in the yard,[3] why on earth would a big leader do such a thing; but actually it's a

---

3. See Guntur Soekarno, *Bung Karno: Bapakku, Kawanku, Guruku* [Bung Karno: My Father, My Friend, My Teacher] (Jakarta: Dela-Rohita, 1977), pp. 115–19.

good thing and quite touching because that's how he shows his spiritual connection with the masses of the poor, something Indonesia very much needs since the greater part of Indonesians are poor, anyway young people and older people who are higher-ups never think about things like these, even though they really matter for the people of Indonesia to proceed on their noble path toward independence, no matter whether independence comes as a gift from Japan or the way the young guys want it who they say often discuss things with some short little guy from Minang who has a mad laugh but they say he's smart like a mouse deer and sometimes he sneaks in places secretly once the sun goes down, in particular along Diponegoro Street where Bung Hatta lives, he's this skinny little guy like a kid out of SMT[4] and his name has "sutan" in it or something, that's right, Sutan Syahrir; so who knows who they're going to go along with, the ones who say don't make a lot of noise or the Japanese will go amok and the masses do whatever occurs to them and then there'll be a bloodbath, so just be good and cooperate with Japan, or the heroic type like that guy Tiwi sings the praises of; oh my goodness Tiwi has disappeared again, where is that girl, for sure she's talking with that guy with the wooden rifle again, isn't that the limit, if you give her half a chance, say now don't go crazy without any brakes, well what do you expect of young people in wartime who've learned how to carry a wooden rifle or wear a dress they insist on hemming above the knees, aren't they ashamed of themselves even though it's true everyone knows cloth is expensive now everyone has to cut corners, but a woman's self-respect shouldn't be where you cut corners, should it? but all right never mind everything's in the hands of Allahuakbar Allahuakbar Allahuakbar.

---

4.  Sekolah Menengah Tinggi [High School]. Now STMA [Sekolah Menengah Tinggi Atas=Senior High School].

So when the sun finally rose on the long-awaited day, what mattered was that Bu Fat had given instructions for providing tea and
snacks for a fair number of guests and very early in the morning the
kitchen got a lot of servant-volunteer reinforcements in order to wel-
come the day's ceremony which according to the youths posted as
guards was called: Proclamation; everything's in order, Madam, the
floors inside as well as in the reception hall in front have been mopped
till they shine, and the gardener got a bamboo flagpole ready yesterday well it's been around for a while but he painted it like new;
and along the same lines Tiwi was warned not to leave dirty clothes
hanging outside, and for the time being don't hang wet clothes out
to dry till the ceremony's over, now you can't go celebrating a historic day with underpants, long johns, and bras, that wouldn't be
right, would it; the important thing is don't forget to give the elec-
tricians who take care of the radio-transmitting equipment something to drink and some breakfast if they haven't eaten, otherwise
the broadcast won't be heard overseas; and the most important thing,
go one more time and check Bung Karno's bathroom and the WC
and the ones reserved for the most important guests, they have to
be really neat and not a disgrace and the one specially for the young
guys and people from outside have to be clean and attractive too so
they'll be happy to use it if they need to and won't go into Bung
Karno's WC.

Say now take a look at that Tiwi, whew is she ever pretty, with
her white blouse and skirt neatly ironed and her hair in a long braid
with two red ribbons, where'd she get those ribbons, this girl is a
cutie-pie, even if she is just a laundrywoman, but her Dutch is way
better than that wooden rifle guy's, the one who goes around bark-
ing like a Japanese officer; but what can you do, if they're fated for
each other they're fated for each other, and if not, well a girl like her
with those looks and those breasts and that waist and that ass, she's
not going to have any trouble finding takers, as long as she's not too

dumb to know better than to size up a man by his wooden rifle, or
that other gun God gave him, but of course no young person is going
to just follow advice from someone older than them, they've got to
do it all themselves, try it themselves, so then once they've fallen in
a heap in the gutter, that's when they find out how much mud stinks,
you know how it is, there's a lot of guys out there really great looking Gatotkaca types but all they want to do is fly around and get
into brawls, so choose yourself some guy like Garèng or Pétruk or
Bagong, never mind they're servants, don't look like much but what
you'll get back is a good laugh your whole life through and you won't
have to worry about keeping up appearances because hey appearances don't come cheap, don't you believe in this world you're going
to get something for nothing.

   But Tiwi's interest was fading waning in the bald young man with
the wooden weapon who was said to be responsible for delivering
secret letters, ever since the day of Bung Karno's kidnapping, she was
so mad and so disappointed in snotty Mr. Seinendan because he didn't
give a thought to the little baby, how on earth could you kidnap a
baby for political reasons, without even taking along a milk bottle
mind you, that's proof he doesn't have the makings of a future father
who'll stand by his family, so this is *sayonara*,[5] and anyway Tiwi had
seen him many times over with another girl in his lap who had short
hair and wore skirts dyed in mahogany bark and a white blouse that
clearly used to be a tablecloth you could still see tea and spicy sauce
stains on it, wearing glasses and she was always carrying books and
a notebook; it wasn't that she was mad or jealous because obviously
the object of her affections was still a kid and what young woman
could respect a boyfriend who was so immature, oh may this ceremony bring in a new age and a new atmosphere including (who
knows?) a new boyfriend who didn't have just a wooden rifle but a

---

5. Good-bye (Japanese).

real, genuine rifle with a glinting blue steel barrel hole that you could put real, genuine grown-up copper into.

Thus it was a truly bright morning that day, with all the preparations keeping everybody terrifically busy, and the reception hall decorated in the middle by a microphone that looked like an elegant little box, more modern than the old-fashioned loudspeaker that wobbled and wavered on a fence post, which later would pick up Bung Karno's sweet, commanding voice to broadcast it to all corners of the world. The atmosphere was truly solemn, no one was joking around let alone shouting like villagers, everything was quiet awaiting Bung Hatta who was predicted to and did indeed come in his car 10 minutes before the ceremony started, getting out of it and smiling serenely nodding his head to the guests who were already assembled. Earlier that morning Bung Karno was still a bit feverish, clearly because he was exhausted and tense during these critical political preparations, but now he came out of an inner room together with Bung Hatta and the other leaders; Bung Karno with his large powerful frame looking dashing and self-assured, while Bung Hatta looked cool calm and collected. Beyond that Tiwi didn't really know what happened, except that at a certain moment Bung Karno approached the microphone and read something from a piece of paper that was folded over; then there was the ceremony raising the Red and White Indonesian flag, which late last night Bu Fatmawati was still sewing together with her own hands, and Tiwi had respectfully asked for the leftover scraps of the material scattered about the floor, which that gracious and devout lady allowed her to take with a smile full of understanding yes, fine, fine, my dear Tiwi, those red scraps would be good for you to make into ribbons for your hair, there's just the right amount, not too much and not too little. Thus in the middle of the night when Bu Fat had fallen asleep exhausted cradling the baby and people were still waiting up for Bung Karno to get back from an important meeting at the home of a Japanese admiral, held no doubt to clinch some important decision, that night Tiwi with

her gracious and devout mistress's permission slowly and without
making any noise that might wake the baby, hemmed the ribbons-
to-be that the next day would ornament the thick, beautiful hair that
is every woman's pride, oh how fortunate was Tiwi to be granted
the chance to be the laundrywoman here at East Pegangsaan Street,
even if she did feel the loss of her enchantment with a young hero
who was blazing with enthusiasm but who in the eyes of his girlfriend was neither smart enough nor accountable; oh who knows,
maybe it's true what Auntie says about how true love rarely comes
with your first prospect or your first kiss; oh who wouldn't be proud,
like Tiwi, to get her first kiss from the very person of Bung Karno
himself, even though it was only a kiss on her forehead and in plain
sight of the sweet and gracious and devout Ibu Fat, it was when Tiwi
presented him with a bunch of jasmine flowers on his birthday in
the name of the household domestic staff, so it wasn't all that romantic like in the magazines, whereas that young guy in the leaf-green
uniform with the wooden gun who blazed with enthusiasm never
kissed her, hey let alone kissed her, he never even held her hand or
touched her shoulder, well that's what comes from his getting
trained into Japanese discipline and maybe too because he was still
pretty immature, he was still a child compared to Tiwi who was big
for her age and striking and had full breasts; it was really the case
that Tiwi felt like with the coming of that important moment in the
reception hall at 56 East Pegangsaan Street, something crucial was
going to come about in her life, she didn't know just what but she
could feel it; something mysterious, something bewitching, something to provide a path to follow and a future for Tiwi Linda Iin from
the Progo and Elo Valleys, eternally lovely nostalgia-inducing rivers
that come specially to Magelang in order to pay their respects to Tidar
Mountain, the nail that fastens the Island of Java.

Indeed it came to pass, that event full of mystery, whose coming Iin Linda Tiwi sensed before it happened: in the moment of silent

meditation, while all those present prayed fervently for those who had sacrificed their lives struggling for freedom, at just that meditative moment the microphone, the very Microphone of the Proclamation in the shape of an elegant, modern box, calmly and authoritatively turned about, then set out, went down the steps of the reception hall, and proceeded slowly in the direction of Tiwi who at that time was standing along with some other household servants under a tree in the front yard, passed through the row of young fighters and the honored guests, then stood directly in front of Tiwi, the box smiled then whispered softly to her, a bit froggily: Speak, speak into me, dear Iin. Of course she was startled more than just a little this girl from Kedu child of a KNIL corporal and a fried-cassava-snack seller, she didn't know what she should do or say for that matter. Don't be afraid whispered the Microphone gently, don't think that the only ones who have the right to speak into me are the big leaders of the nation or prominent intellectuals, speak! Okay but Tiwi's only a laundrywoman. That's just it, that's just it, my dearest Tiwi, speak. So Tiwi said a couple of words, now forgotten. The Microphone of the Proclamation smiled once again: the moment of silence is almost over, I have to go back now. At special moments I'm going to visit you. That's all for now, Tiwi, FREEDOM! Thus the Heirloom Microphone walked back to the front of the reception hall, went up the steps, stood in its original place, faced the direction of the various proclaimers. No one saw the Microphone's excursion because everyone, deeply moved, was observing that solemn moment of silence. Once Bung Hatta had left East Pegang-saan Street, and Bung Karno had gone inside to take a little rest, Tiwi without even changing out of her neatly ironed white blouse and skirt proceeded to the back and started hanging out the wet clothes that had waited their turn to breathe in the bracing air of August 17, 1945.

"Hey, your boyfriend's looking for you, the guy with the wooden rifle," whispered her aunt, but Tiwi shook her head, "I'm not his girl-friend." "What?! Are you out of your mind?" But Tiwi said nothing and kept right on hanging the clothes out to dry. Shaking her head Auntie went on her way, oh these young people, she muttered, what's the point of wearing red ribbons, and plaited ones, too, isn't it to get the attention of young guys, oh well it's the times, what can you do, things change, they change all too easily, the Dutch times turn into the Japanese times turn into the Freedom times.

# Chapter Three

The Republic of Indonesia is not just Jakarta, so it's no surprise that Miss Tiwi took the opportunity to ride the Jakarta-Yogyakarta KLB (Special Train) along with the President and Vice-President, several Ministers and other High Officials, accompanied by all their families and special bodyguards, to look in on her twin brother Brojol up in the hills who on the precise date of last March 4, 1944, the day the Java Hokokai movement[1] was launched as a national organizational exercise in anticipation of Indonesia's independence sometime in the future, got married to a young woman from an isolated village that isn't at all famous and is dry dusty and desertous. Tiwi didn't make it onto the train because suddenly she had become the minister of defense or the general of a women's battalion but because the Government of the Republic of Indonesia got moved to the city of Prince Diponegoro, except for the Ministry of Foreign Affairs which remained installed at 56 East Pegangsaan Street and which was now occupied by a prime minister who was like a high school student who liked to laugh and was irritatingly optimistic but was incredibly smart like a mouse deer, who the people's representatives in the

---

1. People's Organization led by Bung Karno with the blessings of the Japanese Occupation Government.

KNIP[2] and Soekarno-Hatta hoped would be able to tame the Allied Elephant and the gangs of Dutch Lions and NICA Dogs[3] and in addition don't forget about all those native aristocrat crocodiles, old-fashioned or intellectual, seeking their own comfort who were slandering the Republic so they could eat bread and butter and cheese and make a show of drinking beer even though their lords and ladies *van voor de oorlog*[4] had turned them into slaves and houseboys. It then turned out that in actual fact the Proclamation of August 17 which Tiwi herself had seen and heard a while before at 10 in the morning in a solemn and distinguished atmosphere, firm and determined "in the name of the Indonesian nation" if you looked at it closely was well, true and not true: true because that was indeed the way you worked and talked in high-flying political circles which at that time Tiwi didn't understand yet just being a laundrywoman with an ex-boyfriend who wore a leaf-green scout's shirt and a wooden rifle; but you could also say it wasn't true because obviously man oh man there were a lot of people with brown or mahogany or teak or chocolate-colored skin there were a lot of them who actually preferred being bossed around by the Dutch from that colonial Land of Frogs, apparently on the grounds that: being a slave houseboy car attendant felt safer stabler easier-peasier you didn't have to think much compared to wearing yourself out being your own driver following after the Non-Co Republicans[5] whose president and vice-president and ministers had never taken a course or gotten a degree in how to be a president, vice-president, or minister, so it was hard to entrust yourself to them; not to mention the so-called commander-in-chief and all those *"made in Japan"* repair shop officers so they were all wrecks; or for that matter the ones cooked up in our

---

2. Central Indonesian National Committee.
3. Netherlands Indies Civil Administration.
4. From before the war.
5. Noncooperating. Those who did not want to collaborate with the Dutch.

own snack stands who clearly have never shot a howitzer let alone
driven those tank monsters like what the English India Twenty-third
Division under General Hawthorn brought with all those different
kinds of Dutchmen perched on board, from piglet pale to burnt coconut
sugar dark who had those little weapons but they could vomit hundreds of bullets in a single volley and had world war fighting experience against the Nippon Armed Forces who were undefeated but then
were.

At that point actually Tiwi was on an errand sent by her aunt to
buy soap and bluing at the store, but by accident she got swept along
by thousands of people teeming and streaming out of the villages
carrying Red and White flags of all sizes, skinny scrawny sunken-
cheeked and half-starved but their eyes aflame exploding with emotion till their throats went dry yelling and screaming FREEDOM, more
excited still FREEDOM OR DEATH, but some only managed FREED-
or even FRE-; the throngs were so numerous and packed together at
the time that the soybean-paste smell of their sweat would have been
enough to get people really turned on if it hadn't been their goal to
get to a magnetic field called Ikada Square where Bung Karno according to gale-force rumors was going to give a speech to explain what
the follow-up strategy would be to drive out the Dutch and win international recognition; but as it turned out surprisingly enough they all
just got told to go home quietly don't make a fuss to prove to the
Japanese and the whole world that we as a free people are mature
enough to be orderly and take care of ourselves; but in reality in order
to avoid the volleys of bullets of the *Kenpetai* who where guarding
Ikada Square with their bayonets drawn, who could say whether they
would go crazy like those Kamikaze pilots or would get scared they'd
be mobbed by so many thousands of people, no one could predict,
well it was perfectly clear at that time there was clear proof how ready
and willing the villagers all were to support the Proclamation, but the
sad thing was, as Tiwi herself heard, they were disappointed because
they were told just to go on home without receiving any orders and

then they were told to wait and just wait some more; sure there were some orders but they were just from the young fighters who didn't have any authority yet, it was only Soekarno-Hatta that people were faithful to, with a resolve as seamless and round as a soccer ball or maybe a children's toy ball but anyway really heartfelt; only as always it's the elite types who aren't villagers that are a problem, is their resolve just as round or let's hope it's not sort of oval so if you tossed it you wouldn't know which way it would go, joining the beloved Republic or joining the damned Dutch, now that's the real problem; so the text of the Proclamation would read In the Name of Villagers and the Poor, or maybe In the name of all the people of Indonesia but with the added note: except for members of the elite and officials and scholars slanderers-collaborators who need to be tested or bludgeoned into some self-awareness; but granted that's not elevated international-type language, so you can't say it but obviously that's the way things are, it's sad but true but like everybody knows in the tropical forests you don't only find wild buffalos or mouse deer but also a lot of scor-pions and snails and other creatures that only know how to eat and sleep, they don't have ideals as high as stars in the sky like Bung Karno constantly thunders on about.

So once she had gotten to Yogyakarta and the Great Hall that used to be used as the Dutch governor's residence facing the former Company fort in the City of Sultans, and after several days putting the furnishings and clothes of the President's family in order and checking once again the bathroom and the WC and all the little details that the young revolutionaries never give a thought to but are very important to keeping the wheels of the Revolutionary Supreme Com-mand turning day after day, Tiwi asked for a brief leave to go look up her twin brother whom she hadn't seen in a long while. It turned out he had moved a ways to the north at the request of their uncle who owned some irrigated rice land but didn't have people to work it, it was the usual story his two kids only wanted to go to the Tegal School of Navigation. When she got to the village she had been

directed to it turned out her brother's house which was tacked onto
the side of another house plus two of the neighbors' houses were
all being used as a makeshift public kitchen for serving the irregulars and TKR that were flocking there to get ready to invade
Semarang. Her older brother had been picked willy-nilly by the
advance fighters to be the village headman because the headman
before him had been ousted by the will of the people fired after he
was discovered one time to have brought two slices of bread from
the city of Semarang, he said he had bought them from a servant at
the RAPWI[6] camp but the young men of the People's Militia didn't
believe that and in their opinion it was clear Mr. Village Headman
was an enemy spy, don't forget that he was three days late raising
the Red and White flag even though he had been informed by the
young fighters of the joyous news from Jakarta that independence
had already been proclaimed, and even though, too, the whole population was already spontaneously waving that proud symbol of the
nation's sovereignty; so it was Brother Brojol who since that time
was the "Kiblik"[7] Headman even though he was too young barely
out of his teens and a newcomer to the village, but among the young
men he was apparently the most highly educated since he had well
and truly graduated from the *Bijzondere H.I. School* and wasn't arrogant; unlike the Head of the Investigation and Village Defense Division that character Ponyet who would make a talented robber or
ticket-taker on the bus who liked to give strange orders and stranger
still liked to investigate who was a spy, who was pro-NICA, who
wasn't a revolutionary, and that sort of thing, when as a matter of
fact he was in the habit of wandering around looking for honeys and
whores but now oh man was he ever throwing his weight around
because there was a battle against NICA, and here their village was

---

6. Allied Agency for ensuring the welfare of Dutch women and children
   interned by the Japanese.
7. Villagers' language for the word Republic.

situated at a crossroads that was tactically strategically important as the site of the public kitchen but also as the headquarters for strategic coordination. Every night the members of the irregular militias that thronged there in steadily increasing numbers, coming from all directions by means of all kinds of vehicles, buggies, trucks, cars and trains and bicycles, of course these masses of dedicated young men had to have their strategies arranged at Brother Brojol's house which was no longer a house but rather an anthill where the ants' feelers were made of sharpened bamboo, adzes, samurai swords as well as formerly KNIL decorative swords and sometimes real genuine rifles or pistols, and don't forget the daggers all of which were powerful heirlooms. Brojol's wife was still young and he had sent her and their baby to his in-laws far away in the limestone hills, after an unpleasant incident, there was this fighter who looked like a Madurese saté seller with a red-and-white kerchief on his head and dagger ala Prince Diponegoro trying to kiss his wife and do other things that granted are natural but not civilized and against religious morals, so now our Brojol headman by the will of the people was once again living as a bachelor.

Seeing this situation Tiwi sent a letter via a freedom fighter from the TKR who fulfilled his warrior's duties at the old VOC fort facing the President's Palace in Yogyakarta to let her aunt know that for the time being she had to do volunteer work in the village, helping out her twin brother, because things were dangerous and tense leading up to the huge offensive that was going to be unleashed upon the enemy still hanging on in Semarang and so on; the things she wrote were terrifying and it made the hair on the nape of her auntie's neck stand on end, while she also asked her aunt to beg the indulgence of Ibu Fat and Bung Karno and to ask leave from them on her behalf, bearing in mind that the Homeland called her to the field of sacrifice and so forth, akhirulkalam: FREEDOM OR DEATH!!!!

Thus Tiwi struggled to help her twin brother so that the public kitchen that had no funds no budget no nothing other than what villagers call knee capital could keep boiling and frying and steaming, since of course all those guys showing up were heroes and candidate heroes who might very possibly fall on the sacrificial fields like shattered jewels pearls gems or like jasmine or camboja flowers, one falls and a thousand grow in its place, and for that reason they were quick to complain if the rice wasn't white enough not sticky enough too hard or too soft or going off and the soybean cakes were too small or the vegetables had gotten pretty sour and so forth, all this was understandable given that they were heroes and candidate heroes who it might well be would soon fall like one-falls-a-thousand-grow flowers or jewels pearls gems shattered under the sledgehammers of van Mook's, van der Plas's, and Spoor's flunkies, so it wasn't easy for Mr. Headman and the various village officials and the village secretary and leaders assisted by the women and young Tiwi who was only a laundrywoman and only an assistant one at that, to fulfill the logistical requirements as people say now but in those days it was called provisions, because there were indeed no funds or budget with compensatory balances reckoned by BAPPENAS or implemented by BULOG-DOLOG or nonbudgetary funding from clove-scented cigarette factory sponsors or from gambling so completely cleared of religious prohibitions as to no longer be called gambling but rather voluntary contributions, there was none of all that yet; so villagers really had to wrack their brains coming up with a list of who would take turns having to contribute young jackfruit or coconuts on Monday Pon and Tuesday Pahing who would have to put in a goat or chickens and Wednesday Kliwon who would be requested respectfully but firmly to slay a cow for the nationalist struggle against an enemy that had already oppressed people for 350 years; now remember this is a struggle for freedom-or-death because if we fail this time when will we win, and remember that the front line bears a great responsibility precisely because it represents the most advanced front; so if the front line of defense is crushed then everything gets destroyed, because then the NICA troops can advance to Ambarawa once again and then hop over Guava Mountain and pounce down on Magelang, a strategic city since the KNIL had its barracks there in the old days, so that then they could just roll on into Yogya, thus the Island of Java would be sliced into two parts like snacks all ready to eat; thus it was quite clear that this could not be allowed to happen as had been analyzed explained ordered precisely and spiritedly and full of resolve by the *de facto* commander-in-chief in the field at the time that is little Bung Tomo from Surabaya, hey everyone was little he was little the Prime Minister was little too, but please recall Napoleon who was just as little as Bung Tomo, so now this Bung here always gave a speech every evening at 18.00 in front of the loudspeaker of Surabaya Uprising Radio starting and ending it by shouting three times Allahuakbar Allooohuakbar Allooooohuakbar as a sign that this really was a holy war that could not be taken lightly, such that all of the instructions radioed out by Bung Little Guy from Surabaya had to be followed faithfully, because this still young Republic for some reason hadn't gotten a chance to put together a real national army yet; sure there had been generals appointed and divisions created but all that was still at the level of aspirations or formulations on paper, because each and every group's head honcho with a sharpened bamboo stick thought of himself as a free and autonomous general, so everyone had to take don't-mess-with-me-democracy into account because these guys had so many troops; but what do you expect this is what's called a Revolution, so don't measure them against the German army or American or Japanese for that matter, hey every revolution has its own rules and anyway don't we hear the troops singing the revolutionary song excitedly and full of freedom-or-death determination every morning: "The PEOPle have become the JUDGes! The PEOPle have become the Judges!" and so forth; everything must necessarily be negotiated and remember: isn't it the case that the most invincible defense is the defense mounted by an entire populace and remember the fate of the Dutch East Indies army that in only 8 days suffered defeat and the loss of all the territory from Sabang to Merauke because they relied solely on mercenary soldiers who only knew how to go on parade and get drunk on Saturday night; thus even if the official army doesn't have enough bullets, it's clear that real bullets aren't made out of copper and tin but rather according to the Public Kitchen Management team are actually this: grains of rice, and grenades are: soybean cakes, crunchy or soft, and bombs in actual fact are coconuts whose milk is used to cook vegetables, and ammunition is shrimp paste and hot pepper sauce that makes any food at all taste good although the downside is that it makes people ask for more rice. It was really a hassle for Brother Brojol and Tiwi and their associates in the village gathering up all the giant-sized logistical supplies from the farmers who were dwarfed by their suffering, but this was an obligation and there's the matter of maintaining one's good name and more serious still you don't want to get to the point that you're suspected of sabotaging things and get accused of being an enemy spy, now what would that lead to, you might be shot dead by the irregulars who are cowboy brave but don't understand that you really ought to pay for things so that everything goes along smoothly and doesn't break down on the third try; moreover the question remains: who in this zigzag world of the revolution can really grasp the ins and outs of managing a public kitchen without a national budget without a sponsor except for those poor farmers themselves?

Well one day at dusk bad luck there was nothing at all to have with the rice because there had been some soldiers who got mad feeling insulted because the ration was only one fried soybean cake, then they invaded the kitchen and took all the soybean cakes there were, so then there were soldiers who came later and only got served vegetables with their rice; but what was the result? They got really mad because they felt they were being treated inappropriately, no way could you serve just plain rice to heroes; then they accused all the cooks in the public kitchen especially the managers more especially Mr. Headman of being enemy spies who didn't know the value of the sacrifices being made by the heroes and candidate heroes who the next day might well fall like shattered jewels pearls gems or one-falls-a-thousand-grow jasmine and camboja flowers; so Tiwi trembled because some of them threatened to rape her if there weren't any soft or crunchy soybean cakes or better fried slices of chicken or beef with spicy fried coconut on the side because they hadn't come here on a pleasant little outing but to defend the Homeland and get back Semarang that was being occupied by the Dutch and Japanese; thus Tiwi was forced to go wandering around in the dead of night from village to village to beg for help no matter whether it was crunchy soybean cake or soft or dried anchovies or fried peanut dregs or roasted taro leaves or peanut dregs or steamed bean and coconut packets or dried blood or shrimp crackers or eggs the important thing was for her not to get raped not even by a candidate hero.

Thus from that time on both of Sis Tiwi's Arab-Israeli eyes were open to the fact that as a woman she had to have the strength to defend herself, not just the skill to wash clothes or cook in a public kitchen, both from the live-or-die NICA but also from her own people especially the males among them; whereupon she decided to enter a troop of women irregulars even though she was sad at having to leave her twin brother Brojol behind who obviously was just as worn out and missed his wife who had practically been kissed and then some by that freedom-fighter cowboy a while back, it may well be natural but it isn't moral; thus Brother Brojol wanted to go off to his in-laws', maybe it was off in the limestone hills and furthermore dry dusty and desertous but what matters is that it was pretty far from the front lines; whereupon on the pretext that his uncle had passed away he took leave from his young fighter comrades to pay a call there but he took all his money and valuables with him including the potent heirloom dagger from his grandfather on his Bagelen ancestors' side said to have drunk the blood of so many of Prince Diponegoro's soldiers (the dagger, that is) but it was exorcised by a powerful magic specialist during the Japanese period, so that the powerful energies of the patriotic soldiers killed by the dagger were now reversed to become a mystic power supporting those that possessed it; it's true that doesn't make a lot of sense, but they say the magic specialists from Bagelen Magelang are more potent than Mataram magic specialists because it's the Dulangmas area (that means golden palm grease) that is, the Kedu-Magelang-Banyumas region which is rich in rice fields and tobacco that provides the food for the people of Mataram, whereas without the help of the commanders from Kedu not even Lord Senopati in his time could possibly have defeated the Kingdom of Demak, that of course is the version of the people of Kedu and Bagelen who always feel put down because the refined palace types think of them as crude rude dudes from down on the farm because they pronounce their words with a-a-a not o-o-o and use strange old-fashioned words when they mean to say *I* and *you,* and pronounce the ends of words in funny ways rather than the straightforward way they should be pronounced, when as a matter of fact the language of Kedu Bagelen is actually much older much more antique and more venerable like a potent old heirloom than the snotty-nosed kid o-o-o style, but never mind let bygones be bygones, the important thing is that Brother Brojol just wanted to go home to the region of his ancestors, his parents and his parents-in-law and to see his wife Niyah and their child Gatot again, because becoming the commander of a public kitchen and houseboy for the troops' post turns out not to be pleasant because as time goes by it gets less and less clear who's a genuine fighter and who's really just an ordinary bandit except that they're wearing a red-and-white kerchief; and the strange thing is, hey they never go to the front lines, they say they're going to attack Semarang but they don't prove it with enemy rifles they've seized or at the very least enemy uniforms or anything it doesn't matter what as long as it's more than just plain spouting live-or-die but the fact is they keep right on living thanks to the rice and soybean cakes crunchy and soft of the poor farmers who eventually of course get tired of it and feel cheated and then cry out: Oh God, when is this freedom era going to end, begging your pardon.

But Linda Tiwi was different from her brother, she wasn't looking for any parents-in-law or their relatives, she was looking instead for women soldiers who were militant and headstrong, who were superior in quality to these cowboys of the rear sections of the forwardmost front lines, in order to train herself in the military field like Arjuna's wife Srikandi even though she didn't have any Arjuna of her own yet. It turns out it wasn't easy to meet up with women soldiers who were truly as impetuous and impassioned as Srikandi Iin Sulinda descended of KNIL soldier ancestors in Aceh and *heiho* in Halmahera; so then she looked for her father who people said had become a Sergeant Major of the TKR but was fighting over in the Pariyangan region under the command of a Batak together with former policemen and *heiho;* so from her father former KNIL corporal former *heiho* and now sergeant major of a unit that had the habit of greeting each other not with the international military style salute but rather with a fist raised high shouting FREEDOM, Tiwi learned how to shoot and fence with a sabre and the way to throw a grenade and a bit of Indonesian martial arts, judo, and so forth as is fitting for a Srikandi. Her father was very happy to meet up again with his one daughter by his beloved late wife Legimah whom funnily enough she resembled more and more, except minus the fried cassava snacks but bug-eyed in her flaming excitement. He didn't declare his feelings of being touched and overjoyed on seeing his child again with the hugs and kisses in the usual way of civilians but rather by boxing with her, hitting his child's whole body, picking her up and throwing her through the air, beating her against a mattress like the wayang figure Werkudara when he runs into Arimbi, and this was exactly what gave the girl pleasure, she laughed and giggled uncontrollably while being observed by his companions former *heiho* and policemen who were all tough scary-looking guys as is fitting for former *heiho* and policemen who have eaten bullets like they were rice, ammunition like spicy sauce with kicks and slaps for side dishes.

They competed among themselves training Obrus's daughter in

the arts of self-defense and a soldier's tactics on the field of battle. There were only one or two Javanese or Sundanese among her father's troops, most of them were Bataks whom Tiwi was particularly fond of because they're used to speaking frankly they don't braid and embroider and backtrack and reconnoiter when they talk, and they're polite, but of course polite in the fashion of fighting cocks on the battlefield, so they liked to make a lot of off-color jokes and to spy on her when she was bathing but they didn't actually do anything untoward, so sure they could have a little fun in the midst of all that suffering as long as they didn't actually follow through on anything and within certain limits, limits that were limited of course by the conditions of a dirty war, you can't judge these things like you're weighing an aristocrat's hair; and furthermore they esteemed Sergeant Major Obrus so of course they weren't going to do anything to his daughter that may well be natural but is not permitted by the Muslim or Christian or Mix-and-Match or Make-It-Up-Yourself religions; they were rough but they were warriors, warriors of course on the fields of a dirty war, you can't judge them by the standards of a Muslim boarding school or Sunday school, indeed they esteemed and respected Sergeant Major Obrus's daughter Srikandi but still they couldn't restrain the impulse to give her a new nickname: Miss Jugs, alluding to her breasts that were big like jugs but respectfully they never groped her, just spied on her when she was bathing, anyway this was on a battlefield, not a Muslim boarding school or Sunday school, and anyway it seemed like Miss Jugs didn't mind functioning as the Department of Social Entertainment at the Front provided no one tried to put things into practice so hey even her father knew what it was like, the life of a *heiho* and former *heiho* and in any case in the end everything is created by God himself, so clearly there can't be anything bad, no way would God create things that were bad, provided nothing gets put into practice that may be natural but flies in the face of the Muslim or Christian or Mix-and-Match or Make-It-Up-Yourself religions; remember that everything

is going to be judged in the world hereafter, but we live in a transient world, right, what's more this was on the battlefield and in a
man's world, anyway these kinds of things don't need to be subjects
for long, drawn-out debates in KNIP meetings, or else the Allies and
the Dutch will think we're savages; it's not true, they're not savages,
they're just fired up to defend the Homeland and longing to hug a
woman, now that's not evil, is it; so their appreciation for Miss Jugs
was complete in no way to be doubted, but anyone at all who goes
around carrying jugs and keeps them covered up arouses people's
curiosity, but really they did esteem Obrus's child. All the more so,
really all the more so after an incident, well an incident, oh man oh
man how *could* this happen but it really did happen, namely at the
time their troops were making a big effort to block the English convoys that were bringing provisions for the English Gurkha battal-
ions in North Bandung, well now of course *the British* responded
forcefully but they got confused too and two of their trucks and one
jeep ended up getting hit by a land mine; then they, *the British* that
is, fled toward Bandung, but there was one brave Gurkha left in the
jeep who they must have thought was dead but was actually still
alive but only about 10% alive; and because she couldn't bear to see
the brave man's suffering our Jugs cut the handsome young Gurkha's
head off, man the entire jeep was covered with blood; but her fellow attackers only learned of this later because they had to rescue
themselves before they got hit by the volleys of the English machine
guns, grenades, and mortar shells. Only Jugs refused to run and hid
in a culvert, then once she knew all the convoys had gone, she
approached the jeep and looked again at that handsome young
Gurkha.

Her colleagues who had rescued themselves were surprised to
see old Obrus's child pop up out of a gully carrying a severed head
tied up with strips from a banana tree trunk, that Jugs girl is nuts,
but without a word the maiden simply nodded to them then walked
on home, pale tense alone; later it would be said that she borrowed

a horse and cart in the village near where the incident took place, then rode the horse into South Bandung to Kepatihan Street, to the Priangan Division III Command, stopped there, and placed the sliced off head on the Division Commander's desk, complete with the insignia indicating his rank and medals for his service during World War II; thus after that time Tiwi was occasionally permitted to precede the Division Commander when he was on duty, sitting on his car's gas cap[8] to show that this woman wasn't just a cooking-cleaning-and-cuddling slave, not even if it was in the glorious guerrillas' public kitchen, instead she could even take her place on the gas cap in front of the Revolutionary Division Commander; who was unfortunately still called Jugs when really it was Srikandi, but never mind that's a matter of a culture still dominated by males who just aren't ready to get rid of their feelings of inferiority as manly masters afraid of competition; all of that is perfectly understandable and is still in a process of transition, so Tiwi herself was patient and full of understanding for the friends of her father Sergeant Major Obrus who had passed on to her his hormones and virile essences, anyway once again his manly friends were really nice and polite and never "did what comes naturally" to her, even though they often spied on her and dreamed about her well never mind sorry.

But one night after that time she put the Gurkha head on the Commander's desk, Tiwi just couldn't sleep, because of that head's face still young strong and handsome and his insignia and all those medals for his service, she felt sorry for the poor guy, maybe his wife or girlfriend was waiting for him in the land of the Gurkhas; especially once she heard from all sides that many Indian soldiers were sympathetic to the Republic of the 17th of August Proclamation and many turned around and deserted or gave up their weapons to the Republican

---

8. A historical event; see General Dr. A. Haris Nasution, *Memenuhi Panggilan Tugas* [Fulfilling the Call to Duty], volume 1, second edition, first printing [Jakarta: Haji Masagung], 1990, p. 211.

fighters, but Tiwi soothed herself with the thought: oh rather than
the brave young man suffering longer since there was no way he could
get taken to the hospital, so it was better he only suffered briefly and
his head didn't get buried and eaten by dogs or worms or cockroaches
but instead got placed respectfully on the desk of the Division Commander, as though paying the commander a call in the name of the
Indian nation, showing respect in solidarity for the struggle of another
Asian people who had once built Borobudur, face to face with a Revolutionary general. Nevertheless the incident caused a spiritual shock
in Tiwi, should she have gone so far to prove her passionate opposition to the cooking-cleaning-cuddling mentality that she had disliked
ever since she used to get exasperated by her brother Brojol coming
home whenever he pleased and ordering her to sew the button that
had come off his shirt back on and she washed the clothes of this
brother who was spoiled and could do anything he wanted which
was not appropriate for a daughter who had to be neat sweet pretty
polite refined hardworking and ready to sacrifice herself for others,
while her twin brother could play the dumb village kid stealing jackfruit and mangoes and using stones in a slingshot so a lot of roof tiles
got broken. The image recurred to her constantly of the young strong
handsome soldier's face covered with blood with his eyes closed fortunately as though he was entrusting himself to Tiwi, with neither
commands nor accusations, just entrusting himself and maybe even
at peace and contented that he had died not on a mattress in bed or
at the hospital, but in a skirmish in the line of duty.

But what if the brave young handsome Gurkha from the Indian
people famed for their fighting cocks knew that his head got chopped
off by a woman's hands? By a Goddess Durga? Ah, was it true that
Iin Linda Pertiwi had now become the incarnation of Goddess
Durga who used to be the powerful imposing beautiful and noble
Lady Uma, wife of the Lord Guru master of Heaven? According to
the story, one fine day Lord Guru was taking his pleasure riding a
lovely rainbow after rain had fallen and everything was pretty and

fresh. In this ambience of beauty and fertility arose in him passionate and uncontrolled desires and he immediately wanted to embrace Goddess Lady Uma who of course was beside herself with shame and refused, no way were they going to get intimate here they were on a rainbow where everyone and every beast would see them, how could he even think such a thing; but her husband was stubborn to the point well there's no need to relate things any more specifically it wouldn't be good should children read this but what's clear is that they quarreled and the husband abused and cursed his wife but the wife on her part cursed her husband, too, so that the result of this cursing-trashing-goading-bashing at a divine level which of course packs a much bigger wallop than do the curses of lowly peasants, anyway Lord Guru came out of it with a wild boar's tusks but Lady Uma lovely beauteous fair as a white radish with measurements well you can just imagine she was cursed to become a fat lady and a terrifying giantess black as pitch named Goddess Durga, furthermore later she would be ordered to marry her own husband's seed that is God Kala (*kala* means time) and live in a spooky cemetery that smells of corpses, Corpstenchfield.

Lady Uma who is beautiful and powerful and at the same time Durga who is evil a murderer and cause of plagues that torture mankind, oh don't let it turn out Tiwi has to take on Durga's part, this was what was distressing Tiwi when late at night in the darkness of midnight she couldn't sleep and tossed about in her mind, could it be that this is the fate of a child of the Revolution, the child of a time when murder rape and pillaging turn into everyday events; when heroes and bandits are in the same unit; when smart honest statesmen have to sit in the same cabinet with opportunistic adventurers lackeys of foreign capital, when glorious ideals and the nobility of self-sacrifice have to make their beds with the treachery and rapaciousness of those who plunder both property and honor, when noble words and important instructions have to sing together with deceitful propaganda and dirty scurrilous abuse, all of this really shook Tiwi's soul, Tiwi who was still young but suddenly grown up and old because she had been pushed into it by the Revolutionary era; oh does a revolution really mean a war for independence and the struggle of a people, does it mean there has to be both a Lady Uma and along with her Durga? What Tiwi clearly grasped was: the Revolution wasn't as beautiful as romantic magazine stories or radio dramas pictured it, it wasn't as melodious as in stirring songs A Pair of Eyes Behind the Window, My Hero Has Fallen Where One Falls A Thousand Grow, now whose is it and when is there going to be a head that grows to replace the brave Gurkha's head that got chopped off so that it can be returned to his wife or child or girlfriend over there in India? Tiwi got all the more upset when she asked herself whether a woman who has chopped off someone's head can still get married and have a wedding normally and happily, because isn't it the case that a woman's nature is not to kill but rather just the opposite to give life, to store living seed in her womb and to nurse the dear little life, to carry it about to rock it to sleep to kiss it and not to cut off its head, oh who can give her some indication as to whether she is still a girl or heaven forbid is barren having turned into Durga, wife to her own husband's seed who loves to kill people and cause them misfortune? Thus Tiwi wept, she wept tears that were hot and regretful and annoyed and angry and filled with self-hate she wanted to kill herself till in the end she was so exhausted she fell into a dreamless sleep.

In the morning on the pretext that she was going to bathe at the river, Tiwi disappeared from the unit, without provisions without money without anything at all except a letter indicating she was a member of the unit and a soldier's uniform that wasn't really a uniform, who knows where she would go Tiwi herself didn't know, what mattered was to get away from the world of war and killing and burning and raping and pillaging and all those desperate women crying frightened hungry wounded scattered murdered children, who reminded her of Goddess Durga and Lord Kala, but it appeared that Lord Guru's curse still pursued Tiwi as she suddenly ran into a patrol of NICA Dogs troops famous for their ferocity; and of course as usual she was captured yelled at threatened taken to the NEFIS office[9] to be interrogated, that is accused of causing chaos branded a communist subversive terrorist, then tortured given electric shocks punched pinched skinned, then finally yes finally stripped naked and raped as has long been the standard procedure in such intelligence agencies information gatherers since time immemorial and especially in wartime; till Tiwi got dumped as a worthless whore in her prison cell that wasn't really a prison but rather a doghouse smelling of piss dirty and full of trash, for years and years till the day of her release after Bung Karno had succeeded in coming back to 56 East Pegangsaan Street happy and crowing in triumph, but unfortunately without Tiwi's auntie who had asked for leave to go back to her corral in the hills because she was sad always being reminded of her niece who had disappeared. Nonetheless given that well in those days intoxicated with the nationalist victory not a single person could care less about a maiden who was no longer anything of the kind, scrawny skittish smelling of rot and sounding hoarse, thus there was nothing to do but become a prostitute, in the employ of a kindhearted pimp who was quick to see the potential in this body broken down scrawny skittish but still lively provided you put some rice vegetables and soybean cake crunchy and soft in it, especially once he realized that this pleasure-giver in training could speak Dutch amazingly well, so that with a little *up-grading* this NEFIS cast-off Durga could be recycled and turned back into a Lady Uma who was pretty striking stunning and imposing, all the more so once her Dutch linguistic capital, bequeathed to her by the *Bijzondere H.I. School* on Pendowo Street opposite the old Regency Office in Magelang and by her extraordinary genius for learning foreign languages, was complemented with the mastery of English and French, Tiwi went into orbit as a *call-girl* of international repute in

---

9. Netherland Forces Intelligence Service.

Jakarta; and it followed of course that she became involved in the web of international lobbying and espionage, among the parties carrying on the cold war in the days of Allan Foster Dulles, Eisenhower, Khrushev, and Mao Tse Tung, and not to forget the flap about West Irian; truly it was an extraordinary career that took off like a rocket and was particularly fast given that she was the child of a former KNIL corporal and a fried-cassava-snack seller, but that's what every genius's life was like in the turbulence of the Revolution.

Nonetheless starting at that time there was something that Sis Tiwi felt was missing, namely the presence beside her of the Microphone of 56 East Pegangsaan Street, which all of a sudden for some unknown reason stopped showing up to give her strength and offer her the chance to speak into it. When as a matter of fact for all those years full of suffering and sacrifices from that August morning at 10 o'clock the eminent Microphone was something like her new boyfriend, the replacement for that bald youth with the cap askew and the wooden rifle who nowadays people say has become the Minister for Weaponry and Velvet Cap Provisions in the 1945 Ministers Cabinet; ah her loyal Microphone sweetheart from the guerrilla days whom she couldn't embrace admittedly but never mind she could kiss its resonating box and even though it didn't show up every Saturday night for roll call and to take her out to the movies or out to eat that's okay it was still a faithful sweetheart, refined not given to bragging not making a scene every time it came and didn't talk sternly and heroically about the Revolution and demanding 100% Freedom and live-or-die and *Hatta No Musso Yes*[10] and stuff like that but purely clearly unaffectedly discussing and relating about the longings of girlfriends left behind by the heroes of their hearts to go to battle; about the joys and sorrows of the youths who work hard to sneak in weapons from Singapore by bartering rubber and quinine for them;

---

10.   A PKI slogan in anticipation of the Madiun Affair.

about the conductors, station masters machinists or brake repairmen who dedicatedly carry out their duties no matter how many times they're unjustly abused by soldiers and irregular troops, should they ask for a train but there's no locomotive, and if there is one then it's a piece of junk; about the doctors and nurses at hospitals who rack their brains trying to find medicines for the heroes and self-styled heroes, who are wounded whether because of shrapnel from mortar fire or from falling off the fence around the supply house when they were trying to break into it (but the term for this is a guerrilla operation) and steal medicine for so many thousands of malnourished people; about the teachers who willingly teach the heroes' and self-styled heroes' children without pay so that they will grow up to be good and smart and not colonized all over again because of their ignorance, well-enough satisfied if one or two of the pupils' parents provide them with a basket of cassava or a cup of rice as school fees; about the mothers and grandparents who have to stay in the rear of the fighting looking for shelter and their husbands never send them their pay because they're busy attacking the Dutch, but their children keep on crying asking for ice cream asking for shrimp crackers asking for noisemaker froggies and paper windmills and coconut sugar candies and their clothes are torn, and their daughters are clearly about to burst into bloom but they can't get all dressed up like they should, and they were deeply ashamed because all they could do was to force themselves on villagers who were just as poor as they were without giving anything in return; farmers who often had to run hide with their families in the middle of the forest or in ravines because they were afraid they'd get killed by the Dutch accusing them of being terrorists, but also afraid of getting caught by the nationalist youths who would torture them thinking them enemy spies; about lots of people of the same class as fried-cassava-snack sellers who were patient through it all even though they had no idea what was going to happen; about those who were swept away by the storms of the time, a time full of historical import but nonetheless also full of sweat blood and tears, disappointment and futility; and strangely enough, about the families in the far-off Dutch Land of Windmills who didn't actually go along with their children getting told to fight a war against a faraway people whom they didn't know, when they themselves had just been freed from a horrifying war against a regime led by a former corporal named Hitler and another guy named Heinrich Himmler who killed about five million innocent people, that a fair number of young sons of Holland once they got to Indonesia realized what was going on and ran away from the *Koninlijk Leger*[11] and threw in their lot with the TNI even though their military courts threatened them with the death penalty; and many other stories concerning little people powerless people people cheated by political trickery people who are always defeated and blamed by this party and that party so they just cling to God and wait for a miracle while they moan as so many millions of little people have moaned for century upon century, whether under the Dutch colonialists or under the kings and regents and generals among their own kind; so in that time in the guerrilla era the nice Microphone always came and went giving encouragement and good company and for that matter cordially invited Iin Tiwi to please talk into the Microphone about anything she could as long as it was honest and from the heart; with assurances that for absolultely sure everything she said would reach the masses in their millions and listeners in all corners of the world, especially our own people who are suffering and exhausted, it stands to reason because the historic Microphone of 56 East Pegangsaan Street is truly potent and can stir hearts without needing to be powered by electricity from any generator, because it has special wavelengths all its own that are generated by the tremulous longings of so many millions of poor humble exhausted humans suffering under oppression in whatever form, no matter whether from

11. Royal Army (Dutch).

outside or from among one's own people; and that Tiwi must stand straight and strong not waver in her service to the people of her sort maids launderers or fried-cassava-snack sellers or corporals or farmers in the boonies; yes at that time her Microphone Companion from 56 East Pegangsaan Street came and went loyally and came again to divert and befriend her; still for some reason then it hid and never reappeared once Bung Karno moved to the National Residence on Freedom Field and the Bogor Residence and Cipanas Residence and Hotel Indonesia and Yasa House and wherever else with women whom Tiwi didn't know. And as for Tiwi herself?

Well she turned into that high-class *call-girl* because of her fluency in Dutch and in English and in French even if it was only just enough for the business of lobbies and beds and who knows what else; the funny thing but then maybe not so funny was that the Friendly Microphone just never popped up again, at the very least it could have said where it was going, right; how come it didn't give any account of itself, was it maybe that it was disappointed because its friend had become a mattress for anyone who could pay the price whereas in the past she had opposed in principle the cooking-cleaning-cuddling view of women, and for that reason thought it better for the time being to retire and engage in a fast in the revolution museum; lonely and alone together with the Text of the Proclamation that they said was somewhere around here stored in a box of heirlooms along with the historic flag whose scraps Tiwi had once worn as a young woman's ribbons for her hair, ah at that time Iin Sulinda was still a good girl whom Bung Karno had once kissed on the forehead in front of Bu Fat and the household staff in a little ceremony to present him with a wreath of flowers on the occasion of his birthday, just simple flowers from the garden at 56 East Pegangsaan Street, not store-bought, oh they were very different the young Bung Karno and the old Bung Karno, the young Iin and old Auntie Wi Miss Bi of future days; is that really the path life takes, always young and pure then old and stained? Who knows who knows don't think about it too long otherwise you'll start crying again, crying over something that is long past and is not productive and not efficient and not accelerating-modernating what's the point of mulling over things and all these reflections if everything has gotten old and those fighters from long ago have paunches getting ever pudgier and the women can do nothing except gossip, compete for things power sex, isn't it more honest to just become a high-class *call-girl* for lobbying groups and diplomatic espionage who still does something worthwhile, well worthwhile for whom Auntie Wi herself no longer knew because her old friend the Microphone of 56 East Pegangsaan Street no longer paid her calls showing up to give her advice, maybe it couldn't make sense of the times that had become so different either, and preferred to stay quiet and hide and pray; oh well maybe it was Auntie Wi's fault, why had things turned out this way, why had she forgotten why had she not gone to visit her twin brother up there in the limestone hills for such a long time, and asked after his wife Niyah and Gatot and the other kids, what grade in school were they in now and how about the corn had rats gotten into it or not, natural rats and bureaucratic parasite rats; just like what beck-and-call-girls experience too, now how can you call a beck-and-call-girl a girl but anyway it's clear what people mean, right, they often experience pests of locusts and rats, get ripped off by their pimps or *lady chaperone*[12] or whatever they're called or by the shady tax office or a nonbudgetary committee; but what can you do really what can you do, the rice has turned to mush, and her hymen had been broken by NEFIS, so what can you do, that's the Indonesian phrase that fits the best, even if it is from Market Malay, still it's the Malay of true everyday reality.

---

12. Lady spokesperson/escort for a female star.

# Chapter Four

What can you do, all of that was in the past, the romantic young people's Revolutionary past that will never return except in longing lamenting nostalgia-filled dreams that are of no use ... her age had already surpassed half a century, oh no matter what happens in a human life especially to a woman who even way back when in paradise was created from one of Adam's ribs, it isn't even clear which rib, was it the one close to his heart or maybe the one closest to his stomach, but born in the chaotic era of the World War followed by the Revolution, what can you do about it, in the end Pertiwi turned into Auntie Wi then Sis Nus or *Madame Nussy* who forgot how she had once been noticed approached and cajoled into speaking into the Microphone of the Proclamation, forgot how once her two thick pigtails had been decorated with red scraps from the flag sewn by the Mother of the Proclamation who was friendly and sweet and fair and fine and pious; oh well maybe it's really quite normal for someone who since childhood has been deprived of everything to go nuts enjoying freedom and luxury even if that freedom was purchased at great cost by the generation of her father the former KNIL soldier and *heiho* who was attacked by the Allies every day in Halmahera and drifted for so many days on the Java Sea, without being in the least tempted by greed to try to look for and take possession of the five tons of Dutch coins that sank, the secret of which he once entrusted to a minister of finance in the Liberal Democratic era; the era when every month witnessed a Cabinet reshuffle and every week there were generals fired by their chiefs of staff and every day there were more new parties all of them fighting for the rights of the masses, and every hour there were statements supporting manifespolantinekolimpronefos[1] that flared up into *tohellwithyouraid*[2] and every minute there were village devils getting eradicated and every second there were more new potholes in the asphalt roads; so finance ministers in some cabinet it's hard to dredge up which one in the long series apparently sent out a team of human frogs who were specially trained at the base *Firth of Forth of the British Navy*[3] in Scotland, and then sure enough they succeeded brilliantly, in keeping with the seething passions of the *new emerging forces* described by the President Highest Commander of the Armed Forces Great Leader of the Revolution Mandatee of the MPRS they managed to fish up the sacks with five tons of Dutch coins and strangely enough the sacks hadn't rotted but later it turned out those coins did indeed rot the committee that had ordered the treasure's retrieval, without of course informing or so much as giving a little present to the former *heiho* Obrus who provided the information in the first place and never did know and fortunately till his death never learned about the fate of the five tons of things from Halmahera because he had "gone home," besides meeting God especially to meet up again with Legimah the fried-cassava-snack heroine from close to the Chinese temple at the corner of the Magelang town square who was always faithful in a relative sense to her husband and children even though for a little while she did express her gratitude, in her own way, to her older brothers who had nobly chased the Dutch

---

1. Manifes Politik Anti Neo-kolonialsme Pro New Emerging Forces. [The Political Manifesto of Anti Neo-colonialism Pro New Emerging Forces.]
2. Go to hell with your aid! Bung Karno's refusal of U.S. economic aid.
3. Great Britain's Navy Base.

from the homeland, so clearly it wasn't a terribly big sin compared with those guys having a high time with low-priced women in Las Vegas or Amsterdam using diplomatic passports and the coins that according to the Constitution of 1945 were actually the property of the Nation, but well let it go let bygones be bygones what point is there for us to grumble unproductively, because ever since Aidit got something-or-othered by the green shirts and striped shirts around Klaten, what matters is productivity, except for the productivity of giving birth to children.

But in this matter Sis Linda didn't envision things like other women who yield to biological urgings, because for some reason she had thought to herself for quite a while, it might well be that the tradition that kept women cooking cleaning and cuddling should be counted among the neocolonialist oldefos,[4] and she began to cook up the idea that it might very possibly be the case that a woman's pretty face was particularly important to balance the evil countenance of men who always want to fight and bring down cabinets; in fact faces, especially pretty ones, Auntie Wi supposed, were for making a living; and that even breasts furthermore weren't really there in the first place to provide milk for babies because for that purpose modern people were in a position to build milk powder factories, but rather to prove just how wrong Sigmund Freud the Jew from Vienna was when he presented deceptive scholarly disquisitions of doubtful validity, to the effect that women from the time they're little are possessed by feelings of inferiority because they don't have a bird in their lap like boys, say it's just the opposite; if Sigmund Freud who is taught at every university were still alive for sure Auntie Wi would point at the skirtchaser's nose and pull on that irritating beard of his till he screamed with pain and begged for mercy, in plain words, not scientific ones maybe but clearly borne out by

---

4. Old Established Forces=Older Powers That Are in Place.

everything in the Natural World; she would explain that it is precisely the boys in fact who from the time of puberty always feel
inferior vis-à-vis the other sex because they feel that they don't have
fruit on their chests the way every good tree bears fruit, so every
person should be like that too, they should have what it's fitting for
them to have; okay so now what's Freud going to say to that, don't
go thinking *Punyo* Pertiwi who comes from Mt. Tidar before which
bow down the Rivers Progo and Elo doesn't know who Freud was
and what he taught, hey isn't the number of one-day seminars
inflating wildly in this age of communications?

Now as for that very sensitive section of the body that the religious scholars dub the *aurat,* about that too Iin Linda Pertiwi had her
own opinion which of course need not fall in with the conventional
traditional, because old-fashioned ways only apply to those cooking cleaning cuddling women mentioned earlier, who clearly are a
different type of animal altogether from a career woman like *Punyo*
who prefers to be called by her nicknames Iin, Linda, Tiwi and in
later days Nusi Nusimus or Miss Bi in accordance with the situation
and mood. Certainly not, ever since the Microphone of East Pegangsaan Street spoke cordially and sympathetically to the young servant
laundry girl Tiwi has no longer been a cooking cleaning cuddling
woman, but rather active in *nation building,* even though she only graduated from the Sempoerna People's Elementary School formerly the
*Bijzondere H.I. School* on Pendowo Street opposite the old Regency
Office, because in the thundering of the revolutionary wheels as they
turn there is no need for *textbook thinking,*[5] so roared Bung Karno
(unfortunately without Bung Hatta); especially in the Lekra organization[6] people didn't need to show diplomas in cooking cleaning cuddling, what mattered was to have a revolutionary anticapitalist and

---

5.  To follow guidelines inflexibly.
6.  Lembaga Kesenian Rakyat=an arts organization set up by the PKI.

imperialist spirit and to embrace socialist realism[7] in art which of course Miss Bi very much supported because she was not ashamed (at that time) to call herself a child of the masses. Speaking of socialist *realism* obviously every woman (in the Old Order days the term lady wasn't all that common because it was thought feudalistic and Javacentric) anyway every woman is always realistic, certainly women among the masses, not just in the Old Order but for as long as this round earth has turned; how could any creature that has to give birth to and nurse her young not be realistic, from her very nature she has no alternative, just look at a lady's anatomy; so the fundamental directive on which Tiwi made her contribution to *nation building* was precisely socialist realism, only of the Pancasila variety; it's just too bad that at that time their group was manipulated by a party oriented toward Beijing, and not toward Sabang or Merauke or Pemeungpeuk or Gorontalo.

. Thus it isn't surprising if the old Microphone of East Pegangsaan Street never turned up again to approach Iin and invite her to speak a into it a little, so that the nation and the world might hear what she thought and proposed; granted, Iin had once from inside the hellish NEFIS cell screwed up her courage to pronounce with enormous effort and in a weak voice a message or if one could use the term her directives to a UN Commission, Queen Juliana, Prime Minister Drees of the Netherlands, but unfortunately Iin always forgot what it was she had said into the Microphone; maybe this has turned into a national trait we can't get away from even if we'd like to, being quick to forget; but it's clear that she had, with the secret guidance of the Microphone, repeatedly approached Bung Karno and Bung Hatta in the time of the Old Order to ask why on earth did the price of rice and sugar and everything else keep going up, why were Indonesians so happy to quarrel among themselves about things of

---

7. Communist parties' official artistic style.

no consequence, and for that reason wouldn't it be better to have a new Proclamation, so there'd be a country called Java and one called Sumatra, another one Flores, Kapuas and so forth, so that they would all be satisfied and peace would be restored; but Bung Karno told her off angrily but frankly, a republic is not a clothesline on which clothes can be hooked each to its own wire, and that Miss Tiwi shouldn't concern herself with complicated political matters, especially in the face of the CIA which was always trying to shatter *the new emerging force,* and it would be better if she thought seriously about why she wasn't married even though everything about her was ready for it, both her body and her mind; and that the nation of Indonesia would only become great if its population increased like the PRC's, so that the greatest service a woman could perform was to give birth to patriots of the Glorious Indonesian nation, as was done by the revered hero of the Bratayuda war Arjuna who impregnated women wherever he went and had lots of children; but Iin as a holder of military academic qualifications and bearer of the Guerrilla's Star explained to the great man that she was of a different opinion, and that the cooking cleaning cuddling theory actually lowered women's status, when as a matter of fact wasn't it the very matter of women's status that Bung Karno had wanted to champion when he wrote his novel *Sarinah,* even though there were many parts of that book that Iin didn't agree with? Bung Karno laughed and his beautiful canine teeth made him very appealing when he laughed; and truly for some strange reason, at that moment Sis Linda very much wanted to hug him and kiss the Great Leader of the Revolution including the Women's Revolution, but suddenly the Microphone of East Pegangsaan Street stood between the two of them and its box struck Sis Linda on the forehead so that she would come back to her senses and take her leave, but not before she had been given the great man's photograph signed with his gold Parker pen, along with a wool shawl that he had once worn when he was freezing cold in Moscow.

Bung Hatta was more restrained and explained many things that had happened behind the screen that she hadn't heard before, for example that the reason Bung Karno-Hatta hadn't taken part in the guerrilla fighting was because the Presidential Guard wasn't prepared, they had all run away, and about the special article concerning the Cooperative-based Economy that was to become the secret heart of the plan to make the Indonesian people prosperous, harmonious, and mutually supportive; nevertheless while Co-proclaimer of Independence and Chief of Cooperatives Hatta appeared calm he also seemed very anxious and sad when he talked about how the public didn't properly understand the essence of deliberation and democracy, and that the democracy between the years 1945 and 1950 wasn't at all the same as the parliamentary democracy after 1950, so it was very different from the fatal flaws that became evident after the Central Government moved from Yogyakarta to Jakarta, because the democracy of the Revolutionary era fighting General Spoor at that time was a revolutionary democracy set up on an emergency basis and at the recommendation of the people's own representatives in the Working Body of the KNIP; and that it wasn't fair to consider changes at that time as a stealthy coup, because the methods and atmosphere of a revolution are completely different and unpredictable, and anyway at that time our people were inexperienced, so everything was improvised and everything was chased up from somewhere, but even though things weren't perfect still the dazzling end result was that Indonesia won international recognition; and because of that Iin whom Bung Hatta already knew because she often served the great man tea and cakes when he came to visit at East Pegangsaan Street, Iin Sulinda must always seek to be honest, even if the whole nation became bad; but you can be an island of good in the midst of this era's floods and storms of filth and deception, acting as a woman who helps others, and don't forget about women's powers which are usually treated dismissively, because look here, Iin, hasn't our homeland always been represented with the figure of a woman, indeed with your very own name, Pertiwi?

Bung Hatta was a pious man a religious man but not backward-looking and meeting up with him you'd just want to cry, because the gentleman didn't realize that in reality there was in Linda's very being something or other, it's hard to know what to call it, a hormone or DNA gene[8] from Goddess Durga capable of causing disaster, but Linda didn't have the nerve to ask him for advice about that because she was aware that she had taken up too much of the sick man's time already. Humans are never perfect, and even when they fall, inside them God's strength and mercy give them the capital to get up again, that's the deepest meaning of our freedom Iin, such was the great man's final advice; thus Tiwi had to continue her struggle not just so that the people and the nation would be free but so that Indonesians as human beings could become free individuals in themselves. At that moment the Microphone from East Pegangsaan Street showed up and its box clapped Pertiwi on the shoulder and hands, a sign that she shouldn't stay any longer and wear out the Hero of the Proclamation. On home Iin went weeping, acknowledging that for a while now she had been more Goddess Durga than Goddess Uma, more Sarpakenaka[9] than Sinta, because Bung Karno who was Arjuna and Bung Hatta who was Yudhistira[10] for sure neither of them knew that Miss Limbuk-Cangik[11] Linda Tiwi had already secretly married, or more precisely partnered, or still more precisely shacked up with a guy yellow-complexioned and albino who was very ugly but super rich. No love no romance, of course, but yeah well you know it was simply business, or maybe just an

---

8.  Basic determiner of inherited traits in the cell.
9.  Rahwana's younger sister who has the face of an ogress.
10. The eldest among the Five Pandawa brothers.
11. Cangik=a skinny and scrawny female figure who is unattractive but flirtatious. Limbuk=a fat female figure who is unattractive but flirtatious.

expression of universal humanism as well as socialist realism embraced in the new era before the Crocodile Hole Incident.

That phrase "a guy yellow-complexioned and albino" was actually a common euphemism in the time before and after Aidit came along with his atheistic but Pancasila-based philosophy, because it would be hard to deny that in point of fact Auntie Wi had truly and so far only shacked up with a certain number of foreigners, some from Beijing, and then after 1966, from Nagasaki, Hong Kong and Singapore, this was a way of life that every religion condemns of course but what the hell, in the end there was a way out which came along at exactly the right time for Auntie Wi (alias *Madame* Nussy), that is, a new Belief System, registered and officially validated called Accsmo; some people said its prophet was from England America, some said from Germany and Russia, whereas there were some who guessed from Japan and PRC, but actually the answer was simply from Jakarta's Golden Junction and there were more and more followers who were full of dedication and not all that fanatical on the subject of people getting together in the manner of animals because after all they're God's creatures too.

Nonetheless this was hardly an error for our Linda because in her heart of hearts Linda wanted to be true to herself: she felt that she didn't have a talent for marriage, all the more so on hearing the commentary of a certain participant in a one-day seminar who cut in to say that a woman as beautiful as elegant as pretty as attractive as someone like Auntie Wi (alias *Madame* Nussy) in reality it would be a shame if she were to be possessed by only one lucky bastard, by rights she should be public property, such was the comment of the commentator who may well already have been a follower of that Accsmo belief system. Thus in the atmosphere and climate of Accsmo, an annoying tongue irresponsible and suspected of subversion commented: Accsmo means acceleration-modernization but it's actually just: *aji kaluwih sejati manungso obyor* (radiant humans' genuine exceptional mantra), Auntie Tiwi alias *Madame* Nussy moved from one hotel to another motel from an apartment in Paris to a *suite* in Vienna and moved again to a *ranch* in Mexico to a bungalow in Puncak or the Thousand Islands in Jakarta's bay, all exclusive places whether it be Macao or Monaco in any case all full of seven spells to draw the tourists with a *super de luxe* style of life that she learned about from serial shows like *Return to Eden* or *Dynasty* or *The Bold and the Beautiful* that are specially promoted by Indonesia Television to educate those members of the citizenry that are interested and inclined to take on a bit of an international style and wouldn't make a mess of it if they were told to lobby whether in politics or economics using procedures and methods that never got taught at their campuses back when.

Once actually a lady reporter from a famous magazine in the capital interviewed Auntie Wi about this matter of shacking up after the manner of Indonesia Television's *Dynasty,* and of course first Mrs. Perti Auntie Wi alias Miss Bi had to make a great show of getting angry, don't assume I'm a person like that lot how come you chose me as a source, why didn't you choose someone else such as so-and-so and so-and-so, they all know the ins and outs about that; but her anger was assuaged once the lady reporter had asked a thousand pardons she had gotten her information with this address she didn't know just where, and here she had only just washed her hair and was only wearing a kimono with nothing underneath, in her apartment on Batam Island, and that all this was only a means of *nation building,* particularly *woman building* in this *crucial*[12] era of cultural transition, and that sources on something don't always have to have done it themselves; but simply because Mrs. Perti has a lot of links and leads for connections and information and all as is characteristic of a woman with a career of international stature, so it's rare to find a

---

12. Disturbing.

*personality* with such a wide perspective, thus the editors ultimately decided to draw on the knowledge of a woman with such wide experience. Hearing all that, Auntie Wi Miss Bi alias *Madame* Nussy puffed up her chest which was indeed highly amenable to just that, and after ordering a Campari for herself and at her request just since she was having something well why not: a vodka for the esteemed lady reporter, then they blew some nicotine smoke together in the air-conditioned room that they found too sterile. Mrs. Perti or Auntie Wi Miss Bi stated that it was her belief that a woman's superiority and most valuable possession was her femininity; but this has to be understood according to the situation and conditions, don't lump it all together six of one a half dozen of the other, because according to Max Weber[13] and Joyoboyo and a lot more experts whose names Miss Bi had once heard at a one-day seminar, along the same lines as Max Weber who thus-and-such and so on and so forth, all this she explained to the lady reporter (who it turned out once she was asked in return had never yet married and didn't much want to marry because hard to know why but guys are so you know like worthless and if they're worth anything then usually they've got their jobs and a wife already in place and four kids, oh well in that case we're both in the same boat; thus unavoidably the conversation turned toward the issue of women "on the side" and such, only at that point *Madame* Nussy became doubly careful don't let yourself get drawn out because this reporter who had just shown up seemed very clever and shrewd in the way she asked questions; well the main thing is that *Madame* Nussy did not in any way approve of kept women, let alone the League of Wayward Wives and that sort of thing, obviously that was the result of their frustrations unlike Nussy; still we need to be careful about how we define the meaning of wayward and that sort of thing, in any case thank you for your magazine tak-

---

13. A pioneering German sociologist.

ing such an interest in me, what's that? my own experience? Oh that's no secret, my husband is a man from Belgium from Antwerp and works in pharmaceuticals, and sure we're faithful to each other even though we live separately day to day, and all sorts of touching testimonials and confessions flowed; thus it's altogether fitting quite certain that Auntie Wi Miss Bi's message will be of great interest to female readers no doubt to male readers as well; but once the lady reporter had left the room and the door was locked Miss Bi hissed and pulled the pillows and mattress and everything apart and hurled them about and flung them to the floor and stomped on them, in short the lady from Kedu went amok like a water buffalo from Blambangan because for sure something had slipped out and that shrewd lady reporter could extract lots of things like a nurse who scrapes wax out of ears; shit, never again would she permit a lady reporter to interview her, shit, for sure she's some detective like that buddy of Hunter's Dee Dee McCall; you're a fool Bi, you just fell for it trying to get famous and popular by means of an interview but now what's going to come of this; she knew, of course she knew but before long Auntie Wi Miss Bi calmed down like every equatorial storm calms down quiets down, the sky turns the color of copper brass, clouds laced with silver edged in the colors of the rainbow and gentle breezes hum: who cares who cares I'm not an old granny left to rot on the stairs; like a flower turned crimson gold, pluck it now while it still glimmers bold.

Batam Island was too close to Singapore, too voluptuous-luxurious to be wasted like a Buddhist monastery that's hidden behind idols' statues in some peasant religion with no future, such was the opinion of Auntie Nus who always looked like she had just turned thirty, still pretty stunning imposing attractive simply dazzling, zestful and resourceful, a challenge to Freud and his rotten *chauvinist pig* theories, the antithesis of Kartini or Arjuna who was feudalistic like Jogja's famous *gudeg,* jackfruit stewed in coconut milk which may well be luscious, but all the vitamins are cooked out of it.

Different, Nussy Miss Bi was quite different from *gudeg* which should really only be served to people sitting casually on mats along the sidewalk; not at all, not at all like that, Nussy was now *une celebrité du beau monde de Paris,*[14] a putting on the ritz city *des belle mannequins de la Maison de Nina Ricci,*[15] with top fashion designers Yves Saint Laurent or Christian Dior; her favorite *atelier* was no less than Hermès with an address on the Rue des Faubourg St. Honoré with a half-century tradition of being able to claim Marlene Dietrich as well as Jackie Kennedy as regular customers, and the whole *jet-set* group plus *haute couture;*[16] it wasn't just like in those *boutiques* where average ready-made clothes are sold, at the Atelier Hermès everything was truly designed sewn bordered embroidered decorated logoed with a label by the elegant hands *du travail manuel superieur superb*[17] (they cost about $1,200 each, just for regular sorts of things), special for *les madames et les mademoiselles*[18] who the people from Shakespeare's land characterize as *languid and lovely, wispy and graceful, hair long and as black as her eyes, noble bronze skin, a fine exotic nose, generous lips,*[19] exactly the way a gallant cavalier[20] once sang the praises of *Madame Nussy des Iles magiques des Indonesiennes,*[21] when she was invited to have an intimate dinner at a restaurant which according to the expensive and rigorous *Michelin Guide*'s evaluation counted as one among

---

14. Someone who is the darling of the wealthy elite in Paris.
15. Beautiful models from the fashion house of Nina Ricci.
16. The elite group that travels hither and yon on jet planes and the World of High Fashion.
17. Artistic handwork of a very high level.
18. Ladies and wives.
19. Full of longing for sweet love, and whispering, refined and well turned-out, with hair long and black like the pupils of her eyes, aristocratic bronze skin, a cute nose that you rarely find the likes of, agreeable lips.
20. A very attentive aristocratic escort.
21. Mrs. Nussy from the magic islands of Indonesia.

only twelve restaurants classed *exquisite*[22] in all of Paris, that is La Tour d'Argent which has a beautiful view of the Seine River and the historic ancient Church of Notre Dame in the heart of Paris; with its unique specialty of *quenelles de brochet* for which it is famous, a gastronomic blend of milk and butter, breadcrumbs, egg, salt and the main thing a kind of large, fresh French minnow with an extremely delicious cream sauce, followed by a stewed dish of *cuisse de canard de la Touraine*[23] bathed in Bourguignon wine, accompanied by a variety of *fromage gras, fromage volvette, fromage melon, galette au fromage,*[24] finished up with *fraises de la Campagne Normandie*[25] while the melodies of wines of *Champagne* and the *vin superieur de Bordeaux* from the choicest sources, Chateau Prieure-Lichine and Chateau Haut-Brion, lullabied their tongues; oh when Nussy recalled those people in Jakarta who kept boasting of how they liked to drink beer or whiskey, her scornful lips could only arch in contempt and pity for those plebeians, well forgive them who are simply newly rich but have never known anything of what is called the gastronomic art *exquisite française;* and those who don't know the glitter of gala parties for starving children in Ethiopia or AIDS at the Palace of Versailles or the Casino de Monaco, the Hotel Waldorf-Astoria, places where Nussy from the valley of the Progo and Elo (her name card read: *Madame* Nussy de Proguelêaux) joked with Henry Kissinger, Elizabeth Taylor, or Jerry Hall, Mick Jagger, Günter Grass, and Solzhenytzyn, even Lady Diana (only bumpkins called her Lady Di) or else Stepfanie Kramer, Dee Dee McCall, Yoko Ono and too Khoping-Ho, Bagio, and Dorce.

Obviously a life of such extravagance invited criticism and espe-

---

22. Most highly rated.
23. Duck meat from Canard.
24. Kinds of cheeses.
25. Strawberries from the hinterlands of Normandy.

cially envy, but for *Madame* Nussy who felt herself increasingly to be the personification of Magelang's Mt. Tidar which according to legend is the nail that keeps the Island of Java from drifting about casting about getting pulled in all directions by the wind and the waves, all that envy was just farting among the ranks of the resentful who knew nothing of progress, the mental dregs of the servant-coolies who only wanted to live in simplicity and hardship; forgetting that the Dutch East Indies had disappeared and that Glorious Indonesia had arisen with special emphasis on that qualifier Glorious; thus it is only as it should be that the representatives of the nation should step forward as the equals of President Eisenhower, Khruschev or Queen Elizabeth II, de Gaulle and so forth, because our Republic is as big as the distance from London to Moscow and from Stockholm to Rome; and its population is seventeen times that of our former master, the Netherlands, and eight times that of Greater Germany, and one thousand nine hundred and forty-five times that of Brunei Darussalam, and that's not even counting our wealth in oil and forests and copper and nickel and fish and orchids and snails that are exported to France and so forth; so we have to look out for our status; and should someone be so thoughtless as to say that Auntie Wi Miss Bi wasn't after all an ambassador or an official representative of the country, well someone as backward as that needs to be given some training in international diplomacy, that before there are official discussions among official representatives of nations explorations and bargaining need to take place first among what are properly called *lobby,* but if you don't have any international vocabulary and only know the language of Jakarta's Senen Market, sure there's a term for it even though it hasn't made it into the *Dictionary of the Indonesian Language* prepared by W.J.S. Poerwadarminta, but it's ready for inclusion in the Department of Education and Culture's Complete Indonesian Dictionary, namely, Scalper, but keep in mind that these are scalpers of international stature; okay so this is a world often deemed shady by those who don't realize that in actual fact they are the conditio sine qua non,[26] and furthermore *exciting* stimulating for those cultured enough to know their Agatha Christie.

It was in that very world of international *lobbies* that Auntie Wi alias *Madame* Nussy de Proguelêaux served her people and nation whose Proclamation of Independence she had attended herself although at the time, mind you, at the time, only as a laundrywoman, but bear in mind too, it was the laundry of *the Great Leader of the Indonesian Revolution,* so it was soap of an entirely different sort and so was the dirt; it's a good thing it was in Jakarta and not in Yogyakarta, because in Yogya for sure the rinse water would have been fought over by how many hundreds of people thinking it had magic powers, such that it would have thrown off the growth process of the Revolution; thus if Miss Bi thought back to that time, she couldn't stop regretting, why hadn't she put aside one of Bung Karno's t-shirts or really anything at all as an object with magic powers that who knows in some economic hard times could be sold to the British Museum or *Tropisch Instituut* in Amsterdam or to some super rich Mashaji XYZ who liked to own things of historic value and magical power; true Iin Linda did manage to get her hands on an old black velvet cap of Bung Karno's, due to the generosity of her former mistress who was fair and attractive and devout, but she had given that to her twin brother because during the PKI era poor Brother Brojol was broke, because just when the rice plants were turning yellow and about ready to harvest in his extensive fields they all got cut down savagely by hammer-and-sickle people who thought their job was just to hammer and sickle every time the whip cracked; but never mind let bygones be bygones, with or without a t-shirt or velvet cap with magic powers here Auntie Wi enjoyed a good income as a political economic national *lobbyist* although without the knowledge or

---

26.  Essential prerequisite.

blessings of Mr. President Commander-in-Chief of the Armed Forces Great Leader of the Revolution and Mandatee of the MPRS, praise be to God!

Nevertheless with or without the blessings of Mr. President Commander-in-Chief of the Armed Forces Great Leader of the Revolution and Mandatee of the MPRS Auntie Wi was not lacking in important connections, such as for example that bald young man with the wooden rifle from the old days, who later turned out to be an important person with shiny hair pomaded with Hong Kong Night and no cap but wearing a snazzy tie, who it turned out still had the job of courier of secret documents and was a key link in some powerful Intelligence Agency, and who of course, of course still remembered the former servant girl the laundrywoman at 56 East Pegangsaan Street who used to bring him tea and snacks, very attentive to politics and the secret background of the revolution; well sure in those days she was a girl of no importance but now she had become a ripe woman of about twenty-seven years, who was full of magic like a full moon on the thirteenth day of the market-day calendar, full of romantic radiation and whom he chanced to meet on the rear verandah of the presidential palace arranging flowers; not surprising since as a Lekra cadre in the flower-arranging and architecture of public facilities department Tiwi often volunteered to help the Palace Protocol Section, or to play part of the decorative landscape when the highest-ranking foreign guests came; in this way *Kamerad*[27] Tiwi whose pretty ears were fine and sensitive like a Republic of Indonesia Radio microphone was able to catch many informal remarks of those gods and goddesses that determined the fate of hundreds of millions of people in Asia and Africa and other *nekolim* continents as well as other *oldefos;* so it was by way of their meeting up during the historic events of the years 1955 to 1960 that there devel-

27. Friend.

oped between the formerly bald youth now in possession of shiny hair pomaded with Hong Kong Night and the full moon of the thirteenth market calendar day *Kamerad* Tiwi a certain bond half romance half espionage and concerned with international political lobbying that eventually came to implicate a lot of matters behind the scenes which were not without links to such elements as dollars, guilders, yen, pounds sterling, rubles, rupiahs and so forth which was exciting and altogether fitting for an expert who was quite familiar with the handling of dirty laundry.

Thus a kind of *secret double-agency network* was quickly put together, both in the sense of half romance half espionage and in the sense of half patriotic half liberal commercial with money handling functions carried out with very sticky hands (because *Kamerad* Tiwi alias *Madame* Nussy de Proguelêaux and the wooden-rifle secret agent, whose name must necessarily be kept secret because he is an intelligence agent even if it is Malay intelligence, had hands made not of steel but of human flesh and blood given of course to oiliness in the hot humid tropical climate) among all variety of nations and the world's interests in dollars or rubles, guilders or rupiahs, pounds sterling or yen in so many different matters, for example the mounting of the Round Table Conference or indeed the cancellation of the Round Table Conference, both the matter of the Asia-Africa Conference and the neighborhood lottery to choose who's going to be prime minister in this crisis-loving period, or in the election budget or crowbarring the Army Chief of Staff and the Air Force Chief of Staff out of their places, it could be in the matter of the Presidential Concept or the PRRI-Permesta uprising, buying weapons for West Irian, in short in every type of political or economic crisis, in the public display of international conferences as well as the intimacy of secret diplomatic plotting or palace intrigue, our double agents a former servant girl laundrywoman skilled at washing dirt away and a former youth toting a wooden stick skilled at sticking it to people, always got liberally sprinkled or even soaked to the skin with the canals rivers or waterfalls and drainpipes flowing full of dollars or rubles, guilders or rupiahs, pounds sterling or yen, what in particular made them the most slithery of all was the confiscation of Dutch businesses, war reparations from Japan and buying a navy and an air force from the Soviet Union.

So in the polemical debates in the newspapers about who was rich *van huis uit* (pronounced: van hois oit) and who because of corruption, obviously it was never doubted by the Post 66 Order that *Madame* Nussy de Proguelêaux should be counted in the category of *van huis uit* billionaires who were rich because of their *huis* or literally their house/household or inheritance, thus not because of corruption or facility or personal connections and so forth, although here the meaning of the word *huis* has to be interpreted widely and comprehensively, don't opt for the narrow traditional sense; and in this legitimate and religiously sanctioned lobbying or brokering process *Madame* Nussy de Proguelêaux by established international rules of course always got her hands a bit sticky, but sticky in this instance in a positive profitable sense as for example the stickiness that comes from the sap of a rubber tree or the sap of a pine tree that gets made into varnish and so forth; not because Auntie Wi Miss Bi *Madame* Nussy was of the sort for example to sell the country short and so forth, but because indeed the system of lobbying behind the scenes has been a customary traditional convention in international relations from time immemorial, so once again according to *Madame* Nussy de Proguelêaux it was legitimate and religiously sanctioned.

Yes, it's quite normal and healthy, and it doesn't need to be explained with any of Charles Darwin's theories, if *Madame* Nussy de Proguelêaux was grateful for and *enjoyed* her wealth and luxury; first because her profession as a broker in the world of international *lobbying* recognized and supported professionally by so many billions in off-budget funds, was legitimate and religiously sanctioned, but above all because there were theological justifications drawn from religion, not just any religion of course but still it seems like it's pretty convincing, that is a theology or ideology whichever term you care to choose, that instructs us that wealth is Rahmatullah [God's mercy], now this according to *Madame* Nussy is where people who are not theologically inclined start to get it wrong: when people get rich it isn't first of all because they're clever or have a talent for trade or work hard or are full of innovative ideas, all that helps, but it only plays a small part, especially in developing countries where capital and productive capacity remain limited but first of all and above all thanks to the Merciful God who likes person X for example, or more concretely Iin who was the impoverished child of a former KNIL corporal and a fried-cassava-snack seller; so no matter what path they take, like it or not, clever or dumb, our Mr. or Ms. X, or concretely Linda, is going straightaway and without fail to get drenched with wealth and then become the filthy rich Pertiwi Nusamusbida. The richer she got the clearer it would be how much God loved her; and the poorer she got the clearer the proof would also be that God didn't like her; well this was something a lot of people didn't know, but *Madame* Nussy de Proguelêaux knew it well, because there was no other possible explanation for how on earth a servant girl laundry-woman child of a KNIL corporal and fried-cassava-snack seller could turn into a *Madame* of the *jet set,* eating breakfast in bed at the Ritz Hotel in Paris, spending her afternoon in London, the evening in New York, and sleeping that night in Sydney, having breakfast in Tokyo, and always in five-star hotels, in suites of course and whenever possible with bathroom fixtures made out of 20 carat gold, clearly this would all be *impossible* unless of course unless she were very much loved by the Very Great Lord who can afford to make anything happen even miracles, but the term miracle is for dummies, the stewed jackfruit set; so in other words and the most exact ones: *van huis uit* rich, thanks to God's mercy.

# Chapter Five

Nonetheless in her bedroom, actually her grand bed hall to be precise, in her bed, actually in her grand bed platform to be precise, with swan's down mattresses and pillows with layers of brocade that could automatically be made warmer or cooler electronically at one's wish, under sheets of natural silk from Thailand, always stark naked because Nussy was very fond of her freedom even in bed, when our worthy lady billionaire looked to the ceiling with its stucco reliefs in the Rococo Austrian style that gleamed subtly softly pleasantly for tired eyes, if she looked about the room whose crystal windows were covered with velvet curtains from Coromandel bordered in gold thread and lace the handiwork of Kashmiri women full of Kamadatu[1] illusions fantasies, yes when *Madame* Nussy de Progueléaux stretched her body pleasurably self-indulgently luxuriously but in her heart all on her own alone and lonely, thus it was that bored-bothered Nussy often hoped that some miracle might happen; for example suddenly outside the crystal window a long ladder might get put up in the grassy area below reaching just beneath her window, then very carefully without making a sound a Cassanova[2] who

---

1. In Hindu beliefs, the still-all-desiring stage.
2. Figure in a pornographic French novel of the 18th / 19th centuries.

was really attuned to the yearnings of her heart and not just after money, would climb the ladder rung by rung as carefully as possible because his left hand had to keep hold of a bouquet of red and orange roses along with white jasmine, holding his breath he would push the crystal window pane that was always left unlocked on purpose, spread the velvet Coromandel curtains with Kashmiri borders apart, and then suddenly and elegantly jump onto the Italian marble floor while bowing respectfully, now holding the bouquet of roses in his right hand and with his left hand gesturing to the side with his hat of cassowary feathers *à la noblesse du grand siècle,*[3] then approach the bed platform with a smile tinged with longing, slowly kissing her so gently it was almost imperceptible but enough to wake Nussy up, then how much would her heart burst open *ah ah mon noble chévalier que je rêve désireuse de vous!* (oh oh my noble companion, how much have I dreamed longingly of you!) or *How lovely, I know you are coming, my dearest hero!* Or *Nha rak tenan, iyak opo rek dasar maling, maling ati bajingan tengik kon iki!*

Then Nussy would burst out laughing all by herself, and often even screamed in hysterical high spirits but then right away was cast down flung into a profound sadness, such that it wasn't clear whether her tearful sobs were due to her being hysterically amused or abysmally heartsick, because consciously or half-consciously she realized how much her life was now smeared with self-indulgence lolling luxuriously in pleasures that she could never have dreamed of and too that she would never want to give up, but were on the other hand nauseating and empty, without meaning without conviction aside from putting things off and putting things off, covering things up and masking things over gagging her heart of hearts such that it became ever more dulled; what in the past seemed an

---

3. According to the aristocratic style of the century of triumphs (in France), the 18th century.

error now seemed to be required by the times, what in the past seemed improper now had to be seen as an internationally validated form of efficiency, she was tossed back and forth between the orders calls of the Microphone of 56 East Pegangsaan Street that hadn't shown up for a long time now, and the technical practical whatever like people do everywhere if they want to get rich and powerful, in step with a world in motion, clearly this transient world isn't eternal isn't the hereafter isn't the world of the cultural manifesto isn't the world of preaching and prayer, but rather the real pragmatic world like she had learned about in one-day seminars.

Bursting out laughing like that, she felt it herself, it wasn't honest, basically what it said all too loud was how she was split in two, because even though she often yearned for love and a woman's satisfactions, eventually Nussy found it hard to believe anymore in those words sensuous-voluptuous love and infatuation and in growing melancholy and rage she suspected that they were just a mask for animality legitimated by a ceremony, the clever ruse of slovenly males who strut about like roosters making boastful crowing noises but actually they're just asking for help, with their impressive feathers of all colors but they never feel responsible for helping to tend the eggs that their seed produces on the contrary they grab worms from their baby chicks without a qualm; just look at them, what so many of Nussy's elite clients are like, they're really laughable those peacocks who think they have Don Juan's looks, peacocks showing off their fan tails with the shiny imitation mirrors on their fraudulent eyes, but it's precisely because of their outsized fan tails all out of proportion that they claim to their own satisfaction that they are above undertaking ordinary labor; or birds like turkeys that puff up the skin on their necks like a balloon worthy of the gods when they're in the grip of their raging hormones; and every time that balloon blows out with a big boom bang all over the place then they strut around clumsily clunkily for hours looking ridiculous but finding themselves fascinating and thinking that they're impressing the females, really it's stupid savage posturing that can only make one's lips curl in derisive derision, well that's really what they're like all those sex addicts that line up to buy Nussy who is half nauseated but also half hungry to give herself over to surging sexual impulses and couple indiscriminately, then suddenly feels impelled to insult them and make fools of those male chimpanzees with all kinds of sexual tricks, so that they feel mocked and humiliated but powerless, insulted but still they ask for more whimper for more, while they look at pictures in magazines or on TV even on the floor on chairs on tables as long as they can do it again sure they'll do that too; often you don't even have to close the motel windows who cares if and hopefully somebody will see how low a high official or rich manager or powerful general or whoever it is who's so important outside stoops becoming a lowly slave inside who surrenders if Nussy pinches him, panting begging her to do it harder asking her to do it extra till they have to have Fanta or Coke poured over them so they'll get up and behave themselves a little, those robotic old goats, who swagger about at the office or in front of the troops some of the time but squeak on the bed but mostly on the floor, like a cockroach asking to get stepped on.

Really, where do guys get off, thinking they're the donors who provided the rib that got turned into the building supplies for women, when as a matter of fact they're just a clump of tough meat not angels not animals with flat deflated breasts with no milk or even a drop of anything that could give sustenance to a sweet little being; all they have is a half turkey wattle half turtle's head without backbone without shape pitiful laughable but their braggadocio is entirely extravagant, just because all the prophets were males so they think they get to say what's good and what's bad in the world; they forget that even the prophets all of them when they were still babies asked for milk from women's breasts, asked for the gift of life's liquid. Yes it was power Nussy enjoyed whenever she pinched clenched clasped crotched rubbed rolled and creamed those old billy goats till their preening little monkeys drooped, yes women really are powerful as long as they know how to use their organ instrument, and that was something *Madame* Nussy de Proguelêaux knew; powerful like the NEFIS soldiers once overpowered her, tough-guyed her was the term, the term anxious guys like to use who always want to be tough and dominate, when what it means is to behave like dumb monkeys and cheating crocodiles; no, the power she enjoyed, it was practically the identical twin to the pleasure of slicing off the head of the Gurkha warrior which she had put on a general's desk, not for her own sake but for her kind, to avenge so many millions of similar deeds perpetrated by the NEFIS bullies on daughters of Goddess Umayi who wished conscientiously to use their wombs to house sweet little humans who didn't have a house of their own yet, to use their breasts for little beings not yet capable of assuring their own livelihood; yes in the name of that half of the nation that also wanted to gain by the Proclamation made that day in the hall which Iin Sulinda herself had joined in sweeping and mopping so many times when not enough people had shown up for work, who was fated and willing to become a woman in service to others but in return for her efforts was constantly kidded made the butt of jokes insulted spied on ripped and torn, oh well let Nussy be the sacrificial victim let her be the black sheep let her be the scapegoat stamped on and scorned as a wild woman a wayward woman, because in their opinion the wayward ones for some reason are always women.

Still why was it that romantic words exotic dreams in her imaginings always whispered as they cradled her when lonely and alone she stretched listlessly *"ah mon noble chévalier que je rêve désireuse de vous"* with all her insides sighing sadly longingly almost bursting into uncontrollable tears? And was it true indeed is there such a thing as being motivated to take revenge on behalf of the dignity of those people, the people of the womb the people of the breast? Thus Nussy could only sob and snuffle in her grand bed platform stark naked under the natural Thai silk, wasting away like the forest disappearing into the muddy swamp to which Lord Guru had cursed her, Guru

who was in no respect a guru but rather a wild boar's fang worthless but the kicker was he was a powerful god and he knew he was
powerful with his sensuous dirty nose-tingling pleasures.

Where was he now and what had he become the bald youth
with his cap askew and his wooden rifle from the old days, who was
passionate about not wanting the Proclamation to be left in the hands
of the Japanese but who forgot that an innocent baby can't be counted
among politicians you need to kidnap, rough-talking, tough-looking,
he was truly enthralling for a young woman with no experience other
than washing dirty revolutionary clothes, and they separated but
met again and still they kept each other in thrall because the matter
of dollars and rubles, guilders and rupiahs, pounds sterling and yen
got mixed into the conversation; then they separated again because
there was confrontation with Malaysia sending him to Sarawak and
Sabah and Kuala Lumpur on secret missions of who knows what
sort for the Army, so that some replacements, who knows how many,
had to get smuggled in to take the place he left empty whom Nussy
never liked but they brought along a lot of worldly money dirt, no
that's wrong: worldly generators; each of them without exception
deserved the title of gentleman with a single mission, to bring in
money, period; and indeed money flowed like horse piss, sensuous-
voluptuous it looked like beer as long as you didn't drink it, nevertheless Nussy did drink it; she was disgusted at first but humans are
the preeminent creatures in the great wide world, most able to adapt
themselves, according to Charles Darwin according to a One-Day
Seminar; thus what once feels disgusting later becomes ordinary then
becomes sensuous-voluptuous then becomes addictive cocaine an
absolute necessity. Wasn't it thanks to the world generator money
that Nussy managed to get her hands on a dozen certificates assert-
ing that the bearer was not implicated in any way in G-30S and free
of all hammer-and-sickle rust? Still, for some reason the winds of
desire blew gently but constantly moaning *ah mon noble chévalier que
je rêve désireuse de vous;* and indeed yes indeed there was one person

yes one person whom she really did like, well not just that, whom she desired she missed she longed for she loved if there still is such a thing as love, and if there is, could Nussy get a share of it?

It happened, long before that ill-fated October of 1965, at the time when *Kamerad* Tiwi in her capacity as a member of the Central Board of Lekra and a special commissioner of Gerwani was assigned to making cadres of artists in Yogyakarta who it was hoped would become the front lines opposing the liberal artistic factions who didn't like the faction supporting Lekra's official art, socialist realism; a special operational mission for noting down and reporting on anyone at all who sympathized with or were themselves prominent figures fingered by Lekra and the PKI leaders as supporters of *l'art pour l'art* art for art, a counterrevolutionary bourgeois faction that was eating away at Bung Karno's authority and joined in spreading the the-revolution-is-over thesis, when in fact everywhere the compradors were still hiding out helping the CIA and the Neocolonialist gang, and evil spirits like village headmen, landlords, religious officials and aristocrats and of course the brokers who control the means of production and distribution in the hinterland still swarmed about sucking the blood of the farmers and petty laborers; and for propaganda purposes that the single true lesson is just this, that art and all genuine and revolutionary cultural expression must be totally devoted to political and economic sabotage; and that artists writers poets and people of the stage are truly misled if they merely write poems and scatter Rembrandt's paints about and the nation's energy supply, just to dream about the full moon and white jasmine while the masses around them get kicked by village official devils and urban compradors; that paper is still very expensive and can't be scattered about just to express art for art's sake that's ivory tower wasteful, thus every square centimeter of paper has to serve total reordering, *Umwertung aller Werte,*[4] and what is easy

---

4. The Reordering of All Values.

to understand and needed by the dirt poor masses; thus national reconstruction lies only in socialist realism which doesn't play around at pretend philosophy abstract art imported from the West's existentialism decadence but is instead dialectical real.

Thus Nussy had to get the process in motion that would tear art apart and make it responsible for serving the Revolution in the city that was once the capital of the Republic of Indonesia which according to Lekra ideology was still feudalistic bourgeois slowly-but-surely as slow as a cart with a shamefully scrawny horse; its populace only liked sticky sweet coconut sugar from Bantul that's too cloying too sweet, a poison to lull the proletariat to sleep that on the contrary needs more dialectic constructive nutrition, and worse *emping* crackers, the very symbol of the decrepit aristocracy, and of course stewed jackfruit, that vegetable marijuana of the aristocracy's dreams all of whose vitamins have been drained away; and don't forget batik cloth and those womanish *surjan* shirts in drag queen colors men wear that do not in any way exhibit heroism and revolutionary virility, the same goes for *blangkon* headgear that actually expresses the aristocrats' contempt for the lowly masses, because in actual fact blangkon were plain simple headcloths originally solid blue-black, but then they got molded styled layered like a layer cake stuck stiffly together without any rebellious passion, a symbol of fixity and the pretensions of the feudalistic types who feel superior to the dirt poor masses; thus *Kamerad* Nussy brought instructions to boycott the displays by the Palace soldiers whose outfits according to the aesthetic tastes of Lekra were hopeless, showing just how much the aristocrats had the mentality of slaves, insecure and dependent, wanting to imitate Dutchmen's clothes but not getting it right and trying to copycat but getting it wrong, so these worn-out soldiers' uniforms were all hopelessly mixed up halfbreed and laughable, how on earth could a cap be called *pacul gowang* [chipped hoe] and military jackets flap open unbuttoned revealing their disgraceful sagging bellies on top of their matchstick legs with outsized boots and breeches that are floppy and shapeless too; with rifles from Governor General Guntur Daendels' time who made the strategic Post Road going along Java's shore so that the whole island could be easily colonized and wiped out should there be any spark of rebellion in any region, in fact that's the era the palace troops' mind-set actually comes from; how could they possibly attack an enemy with a quid of tobacco and sloppy betel spit in their mouths, just look and see how they line up looking like dithering ducks like someone who's just lost at gambling; and indeed the kings of Java and all of Nusantara all of them lost at gambling against the Dutch, just because they quarreled among themselves and fought over women, even though they already had plenty of concubines; well so those were *Kamerad* Tiwi's instructions as a member of the Lekra Central Board and a special commissary of Gerwani at that time, when the counterrevolutionary elements imperialist colonialist stooges alias CIA were fanning the flames of the Cultural Manifesto crisis.

Yet at that time, maybe as a result of Mataram's mystic atmosphere on a Friday Kliwon, one evening when it was already dark *Kamerad* Tiwi was lost southwest of the palace near the Bird Market and was tired from wandering around by herself within the palace's outer walls, a neighborhood that's confusing like a labyrinth, just to learn about the atmosphere at the heart of Mataram traditions so she sat down to rest for a while before inquiring whether and where at this time when it was already dark she might still get a pedicab that could take her back to the Gerwani hostel; well at that moment the young man she hailed startled her so much, she almost stopped breathing and didn't know what to do, as though she were under a spell making her go limp facing the young person she had just met, because that youth oh who would have guessed who would have believed it looked exactly but really precisely the spitting image in almost all respects like the Gurkha officer whose neck she had slit back in the Hallo-Hallo Bandung days when everything got burnt to the ground; how was it possible how could it be, was it really the case that people from India did get reincarnated sometimes like she had once heard in *Mijnheer* Van Gelder's geography class lessons at the *Bijzondere Hi.I. School* on Pandawa Street opposite the former Regency Office in Magelang? Tiwi saw a thousand stars and the next thing she had passed out and fallen into the arms of the youth who looked like the officer from India.

Actually that term Gurkha officer is wrong, because Gurkhas have complexions like assimilated Chinese, their eyes are slanted like President Marcos's and they're square-jawed like people from Samosir Island, they're not all that tall and their body type is slender, and they don't have really long straight noses like rod puppets or shadow puppets, and Gurkha soldiers rarely become officers. The officer's head that she had put on the general's desk didn't have a face of Ferdinand Marcos's sort but was truly the classic Aryan[5] type like shadow puppets, fair-skinned with a straight nose thin lips a perfect oval-shaped face, fine pitch-black wavy beautiful hair, in a word a classically handsome face like the incarnation of Wishnu in young Krishna. Oh Lord, *Kamerad* Tiwi cried out from within her heart even though officially she was an atheist, who are you, once she regained consciousness and looked at the face of an older woman with white hair but with lines on her face that spoke for the beauty of her soul; and behind her was the noble youth whose neck dear God had she once slit? No. He was a youth who lived in the noble city of Yogyakarta but he was Balinese by origin, a young painter (oh 10 years younger) who was talented but didn't have money to buy canvas and paint, such was the account *Kamerad* Tiwi got later, although at the time he was just the deceased Indian officer who rose up out of the pool of bittersweet memories of long ago; bitter because she had been obliged to do something so despicable, sweet because her motive at the time was really just to lessen the suffering of that officer

---

5. High warrior group in India, brave handsome strapping humans.

who was already beyond help, bitter because she had had to act like Betari Durga, and sweet because elements of Goddess Umayi were still present, even though in a spiritual conflict and fury that could never be completely assuaged as long as humans live in this middle world of *ngarcapada*[6] between Heaven and the Underground World; between the palace of Lord Wishnu who rode the great Jetayu bird and the dark pits in the ground the territory of Lord Basuki, the god of the snakes and dragons; between free and sovereign spirits and the material world that tethers and binds.

So it was a complete washout Lekra's cultural mission that had been placed upon the shoulders of the distinguished Gerwani special commissary member of the Lekra Central Board *Kamerad* Tiwi whose knowledge of art and culture wasn't actually all that deep, after all she had only graduated from the Sempoerna People's Elementary School which was a Japanese stop-gap continuation of the *Bijzondere H.I. School* on Pendowo Street opposite the old Post Office; because she just couldn't stand it, he was like a magnet with a million volts this poor young painter who was 10 years younger than she, Rohadi was his beautiful name, Rohini his mother's name, Klungkung in Bali was where he was born but Mataram was where he liked to live, the worthy One who had absorbed *Kamerad* Tiwi's attention, her fantasies and her journey so then she had to keep making up all these excuses to get to go back again and yet again to Yogyakarta Hadiningrat, just in order to meet and chat with him, so that they could look at each other gauge each other evaluate estimate esteem each other sing to each other smile and finally kiss each other hug each other, in Yogya's formal noble atmosphere still branded aristocratic bourgeois anti-revolutionary slavish neocolonialist imperialist lackeys of the CIA. Clearly the attractive force that pressed cheek to cheek lips to lips and other parts to other parts were

---

6. Middle World (Earth) in Javanese mythology.

partly the results of *old established forces* within human selves yet still at the same time were new creations, *new* yes *new emerging forces,* truly *new,* altogether new for Tiwi even though every young lady young maiden or darling daughter from the Horse Cart Town of Yogya with its hopelessly scrawny horses had experienced them for centuries; and fortunately with the smiling blessings and a nod full of understanding from the white-haired lady with the pretty, spiritual, refined face like the face of R. A. Kartini had she grown old and become a grandmother; still in the shadows of him, too, the unlucky Indian officer, whose head had to be placed on a desk in order to show respect to the revolutionary general, with a status far more exalted than if it were left rolling around on the dirty, potholed road full of guerrillas' traps, just to be eaten by ants cockroaches or black crows with their scary screeching; *ah mon noble chévalier, que je rêve désireuse désireuse de vous, que je rêve de vous.* So every bit of Lekra's canvas and Rembrandt paints *Kamerad* Tiwi could steal from Lekra's drawers, and all the inflated money that she could divert from Gerwani Central's headquarters she kissed she sent she shipped to the painter with the dark, handsome Indian face who was 10 years younger than she in Yogyakarta Hadiningrat, which was feudalistic counterrevoluionary and polluted with the climate of the neocolonialist imperialist West's *l'art pour l'art,* say was Lekra right? Because according to Rohadi, he and his friends were just a group demanding the freedom to create like anybody else and honestly, they really cared, they really had deep humanitarian feelings about the sufferings of the people around them, only they did so using the language of art; so who gave a damn about ideology and employers' organizations, Tiwi just went her own stubborn way because love and lust and affection were a lot older and more revolutionary and could defeat anything, even death.

Because he was from Bali Rohadi couldn't pronounce *t* properly but this only increased the fascination he held for her. So *Kamerad* Tiwi became Ziz Thiwi, and it was from Rohadi that Ziz Thiwi

learned to zee the difference bethween nathuralizm and imprezzion-
izm and exprezzionizm, whath the mind-zeth was of Bazuki Abdullah and whath zorth of zoul inspired Affandi and Zoedjojono, to zeek
zenze and meaning in the way shadow puppets, rod puppets, and
narrative scrolls are painted, to learn thath red is not always just red
and thath blue is noth always blue, to ztudy the language of hyp-
nothically powerful maskz that often shake magically and much else.
Thus Tiwi was astonished at how just a few brushstrokes really could
speak and whisper moan and laugh like a madman, a world that turns
out to be more real than the real one we see with our naked eyes,
because humans never see with the organ of the eye as though it
were a camera with a glass lens and regular celluloid film: everything
gets mindlessly recorded and copied but with feeling with sensibil-
ity with tradition with religion with an entire point of view with
the desires and yearnings of one's heart, with interpretations and sentiments and imposed meanings, with both a look on one's face and
even angry teeth-gnashing; so lucky Sis Tiwi could sink into the lake
of paintings of Rohadi's world which in reality weren't paintings but
beliefs, not canvases and paints but rather the soul and traits of their
human creator himself, that is Rohadi himself; thus only then did Sis
Tiwi understand how the whole wide world actually asks to be
painted in order to capture its spirit so that it can live giving contents
to humans' thinking, gestured expressed enlivened such that it
becomes a part of humans, and by the same token so that humans
may become a part of nature raised higher than mere nature alone;
how painting and human livelihood more generally in reality are not
just a skill or what's called a profession, a simple instrument with
which to become enslaved to one ideology or truth that is really only
a little fragment but taken to be whole, but rather a raising up a civ-
ilizing of humans, a raising up of humans' status-prestige and self-
realization; here take a look at those classical *serimpi* dancers so refined
they look like they no longer have bodies of flesh and bone but are
purely immaterial spirits, and look too at their colleagues who are

giving Balinese dance lessons and playing King Dasamuka who is crude and has a hair-trigger temper like a hungry lion; one is like the elegant Wishnu the calm Arjuna and the other gasping with Lord Basuki's sea-dragon's disposition; isn't it true that such beautiful representations could only stem from superior creatures?

Rohadi didn't join the organization of independent humanist artists, nor did he later join in signing the Cultural Manifesto so much hated by Lekra-Gerwani-PKI; it wasn't that he didn't sympathize with this group, nor was it that he was afraid of getting branded as reactionary or in thrall to the West, but because he didn't feel called upon to have a party or a manifesto; this was a side of him that *Kamerad* cadre-maker Tiwi criticized him for, that he was still too individualistic, he should take sides, whether that of Lekra or the humanists, and don't just sit there as a spectator here the point of painting is in order for your paintings to be seen and esteemed or scorned by the people, Rohadi couldn't just be painting for himself could he; her new friend acknowledged this criticism as valid, furthermore once he knew that Sis Tiwi was actually a Lekra person, Rohadi declared that he did indeed sympathize with the socialist realism crowd, because that stuff was easy for anyone on the street or in a coffee stall or even primary school kids to understand; and that both realism and naturalism were still useful at a level like this one of people's actual development, when Indonesians are not yet full-grown and are still at the level of coolies or maids only recently freed from their chains, and because of that certainly can't all be expected to think about and aspire to abstract and sublime feelings approaching a fully free and creative philosophy of art; still don't let one ism get taken to be an absolute, turning it into a god in control of everything, because among the people there are some already capable of aspiring to sublime and abstract feelings and are ready to fly, even if not yet like a garuda well then like a little bird in the rice field or a crow or a cockatoo, that is they're ready to get away from "realism" swamps and "socialism" jungles; so look Sis Tiwi imagine if you were a bird, a weaverbird or a seagull, then the earth would be different, wouldn't it, the patterns of the yellow-green rice fields and the mirror of the lake's basin reflecting the white clouds in the sky, wouldn't all that represent a beautiful abstract painting, and not "socialist realism" in the form of water garbage and mud and grass and stone as people experience them who are still obliged to stand on the dikes between rice fields or muck around in the mud, isn't that right Sis Tiwi; surely you as a woman are all the more able to sense that because a woman is good at learning not to look at a baby's poop and pee as just disgusting filth, but as a bit of the baby whom she loves, and because of that can think abstractly about something that physically really is disgusting but thought about intellectually or spiritually can be seen as an invitation to love, and in this way the bad smell of poop and the baby's acrid pee are no longer like what a man's nose senses or especially a womanizing man's, isn't that right Sis Tiwi? Thus her eyes glistened with tears this handmaiden of Lekra-Gerwani as she took pleasure in Rohadi speaking like this with kind words, with a deep voice, seriously analytically but not disparagingly, smiling with those classical features of Sri Krishna from India's mythology at once ancient and eternal; so that in the end worthy Iin in the depths of her long-buried soul could only respond not with words which would be inadequate in any case but by laying her head on the chest of this young painter who turned out to be much more of a feminist than she was herself, who knows whether because of the fact that she had once slit the throat of a young warrior who looked a lot like Rohadi, from a country that had once bequeathed a noble culture to her homeland, and which would not necessarily agree with Lieutenant General Hawthorn the general of the cactus-khaki Allies about waging war against the freedom fighters; so Iin could only weep because she felt herself adrift having lost her footing and handle on things and the air to breathe and any point of view, as a result of the situation, a victim of circumstances, a means to ward off the evil of the times, the child of a former KNIL corporal and *heiho* and the fried-cassava-snack seller on the side of the road opposite the Chinese temple on the corner of the town square that once witnessed Prince Diponegoro's capture through treachery; yes the city of Magelang which for dozens of years was the colonial barracks but which in its heart of hearts was friendly and didn't have a lot of arguments, because it felt safe prosperous living in the midst of the fertility of the Progo and Elo Valleys, with that funny symbol Mt. Tidar as the nail securing the Island of Java. But concerning the incident of slitting the Indian officer's neck back when, Miss Gerwani was silent in a thousand languages, ashamed and worried that she would be chased away from Rohadi's skinny but welcoming chest and whom she felt to be a lover of complete beauty and peace, at once impressionist and expressionist and also naturalist, appreciating socialist realism but without forgetting the abstract and symbolic layered levels of things; who was poor in money but spiritually rich, as was appropriate for this combination of Balinese stoneworker's son and the cultural atmosphere in Yogya with all its historical experiences granted feudalistic and too refined, such that its artistic and cultural expressions were far removed from the wants of the dirt poor masses, so discriminatory and the sort of thing Lekra's goddess Durga didn't like, who actually was none other than the beautiful Goddess Umayi who was a mother and all, here in *ngarcapada jagad gede jagad cilik*,[7] yes Goddess Umayi who rejected an intimate embrace on the rainbow because she still had some self-respect, you can't be serious making love on the world's parade stand, behaving righteously yet got cursed to become so ugly, to become the guardian of the Cemetery that Stinks of Corpses; well really men are just like Lord Guru, at least Javanese men, but it might just be all men are like that; only Rohadi yes Rohadi who's different who's an exception who's ready to mount the rainbow parade stand bridge yet still appreciate the socialist realism of unlucky Iin Sulinda Pertiwi who once slit

---

7. Earth, big world little world.

the neck of a warrior officer from the country that was the source of
the philosophical and mystical Mahabarata and Ramayana, a woman
sadly who felt herself cursed to be Durga who had to marry Lord
Kala the seed of her own husband. How much this woman Tiwi
wanted to longed to offer her lap to Rohadi, not for the satisfaction
of lust, but rather as a sign of thanks and gratitude to him, but every
time she said to herself: now, yes now, straightaway Lord Kala
whipped her, yes Lord Kala who symbolizes Time's authority and is
at the same time the Witness of Time, with gruff nauseating whispers: hey those NEFIS toughs messed you up, remember?; thus feelings of shame yes shame drove her back into fear: don't please don't
let Rohadi know that I got ripped open, thus Pertiwi was obliged to
act a part as though she were a maiden who knew about virtue and
would not do that one thing with someone who was not yet her husband, even though in this matter her Gerwani *kameraden* for once
weren't all that fanatical, and even though sometimes Rohadi like any
young person asked her for it, maybe because his desire got aroused
since they were in such intimate contact, but maybe because he was
propelled by a kind of aesthetic cast of mind that wished to taste
beauty in a concrete manner in Sis Tiwi's body, never mind that she
was 10 years older, but it has to be said that she was still pretty appealing imposing attractive, she could be a model for the artist Basuki
Abdullah, said Rohadi, but with one thing more, that is her spirit soul
courage life force that moved and spoke that smiled and wept that
yearned and denied, which was clearly impossible in a painting even
one produced by the supernaturalist god Basuki's hands. Still Sis Tiwi
wasn't fanatic in the matter of sexual difference the way most Gerwani cadres tended to be, and occasionally she freely and happily
fulfilled her friend's aesthetic need to admire and more than admire
her pretty appealing imposing attractive body, minus that one thing,
which surely yes surely she would also have yielded if it hadn't been
for that gruff voice of Lord Kala who kept bugging her with the word
NEFIS! NEFIS! which made her despairing suicidal, the feeling of

shame holding Javanese so much more in thrall than the voice of reason or the voice of their hearts.

Thus Sis Gerwani kept her status as a virgin before her friend
Rohadi, while of course Rohadi always kept his status as a youth,
because males enjoy a special privilege from Lord Guru in that they
never lose their virginity, no matter even if they turn into a pisspot
full of leaks from overuse in Macao's dirtiest red-light district. In this
way this one Lekra mission in Yogyakarta was going along swim-
mingly ecstatically and the reports going off to Jakarta always
asserted that things were in order, everything was in order, everything was under control, so the Lekra Central Management with the
support of Gerwani Headquarters felt satisfied, then decided to post
*Kamerad* Nussy to the stewed jackfruit city permanently, and even
suggested that *Kamerad* Pertiwi try to get official identity papers in
one of the neighborhoods of that feudal bourgeois reactionary anti-
revolutionary city so that the various adherents of free creative
humanism could get wiped out as fast as possible; because don't forget Mother Pertiwi was late in her pregnancy, the final outburst was
about to take place with a courier's added note that thousands of
automatic weapons and all sorts of mortar and grenades had come
into Halim Airport to arm the 15 million pillars of the revolution of
the Fifth Force; thus final preparations had to be completed and so
forth and so on and so forth and so on. The truth be told Tiwi didn't
actually quite get the meaning of "Mother Pertiwi was late in her
pregnancy," she thought since Pertiwi was her name that she was
getting talked about and teased; thus she wrote angrily to headquarters that these provocative rumors were obviously coming from
the CIA or maybe even from the Gilchrist Documents,[8] that she was

---

8. Documents said to have been discovered by Vice-Premier Soebandrio's Intelligence Agency from the English Ambassador that caused
   an uproar.

not in the least bit pregnant, and that any steps she might take to become pregnant or not would certainly already have been reported to the leadership were that the case because she was a cadre of revolutionary discipline and she knew the risks of struggling for the sake of the dictatorship of the proletariat and so forth and so on; all that was just to fool her superiors in Jakarta so they wouldn't find out she was sweethearts with an artist that Lekra certainly wouldn't approve of, even though he wasn't a signer of the Cultural Manifesto and despite the fact that he could appreciate socialist realism; *Kamerad* Tiwi still felt ticked off because here it had been spread around that someone named Pertiwi was late in her pregnancy, when as a matter of fact she wasn't, not even early in her pregnancy, when as a matter of fact she was still pure and a virgin to her boyfriend even though not in a biological physical sense but in her mind and behavior which was a much more spiritual more noble more superior sense than a plain biological one. Thus Gerwani Headquarters and the Lekra Central Management had to send a special courier to Yogya to *clear* things up and explain in whispers in the middle of the dark night in a hut in the middle of the rice fields far from human activity, that what was meant by "Mother Pertiwi is late in her pregnancy" was something else and that very soon, before the Armed Forces Day of October 5, 1965, that something was sure to happen just what was still being kept secret but everything had to be in Level 1 readiness; and that the anti-neocolonialist pro–dirt poor masses revolutionary forces had found out all of the Council of Generals' secrets, and that *Kamerad* Pertiwi had to prepare all necessary details and devices in this the Republic of Indonesia's former capital, which only appeared to be slowly-but-surely and stewed jackfruit without vitamins in spirit, but real Javanese people are always hard to fathom from the outside, and furthermore don't forget, don't forget that what comes in for praise in Yogyakarta isn't just Mistress Roro Kidul but also Old Man Pétruk Mt. Merapi, and this volcano from far away just looks calm cool accommodating and beautiful peaceful serene but once it's got to go watch out it just does what it wants no quarter given, it craps on everything lava turds and hot farts and all kinds of disasters that a mountain like that can produce (which of course neither Tanjung Priok Bay nor Kramat Raya nor Halim Airfield can produce); so look sharp and if need be implement Ken Dedes's tactics because the people of Mataram and the Javanese more generally are filth and their cocks always want to crow every minute even in the middle of a sacred reception, and they have no qualms about grabbing worms from their chicks if they're hungry, so the aim of purifying all paths, as long as it's for the sake of the Revolution which (this is just between us) is led not by that Great Leader of the Revolution Mandatee of the MPRS and Highest Commander of the Armed Forces of the Republic of Indonesia wearing the dark glasses, but by the *new emerging forces* revolutionary powers; and no doubt about it, *Kamerad* Pertiwi is one of the important and key figures in the stirring up of those *new emerging forces.* Thus the courier from Lekra Gerwani Headquarters disappeared into the darkness of the rice fields, without forgetting to leave behind a heavy sack which looked on the outside like it only contained shrimp crackers, but which turned out to contain millions of rupiah for the upcoming "Mother Pertiwi Is Late in Her Pregnancy" secret operation.

# Chapter Six

Still in the days leading up to what the candidate dictators of the proletariat called the Lying-in Day of Mother Pertiwi Who Is Late in Her Pregnancy, *Kamerad* Tiwi was in Beijing as a member of a unit with a special duty to help oversee and count a certain number of shipments among the hundreds of thousands of guns that were to be sent to arm the 15 million people known as the 5th Force, farm laborers and others deemed pillars of the Revolution, in the name of the Gerwani women's organization as a female presence because even a woman, provided that she be from among those segments of the people on a level with fried-cassava-snack sellers, was a vital one of those pillars of the Revolution. Thus it had already become routine among *"local army friends"* in Beijing to take guests in their free time to visit the 4,000-km-long Wall of China and see the famous luxury palaces in the Forbidden City, the heart of Beijing, the place where the Manchu Emperors sat on the throne for so many centuries on top of the Chinese people of Han origins; also to the Summer Palace of the Empress Dowager on the shore of a lake that was really astonishingly luxurious, bearing historical witness as to how great and reliable Bung Karno's allies were in the Jakarta-Beijing axis, and how much it was the very moment for every revolutionary pioneer who could do more than just make speeches and discuss things in the bourgeois style to take concrete action. The

Forbidden City is the name of a very large "neighborhood" sur-
rounded by superhigh walls, containing palatial buildings both
mighty and imposing, the heart of the very big Nation of China with
a population of over a billion and a culture that can be traced
through a 6000-year history. To *Kamerad* Tiwi's eyes those palace
buildings looked like the Chinese temples she had seen in Java but
giant-sized and without compare; and of course automatically our
fair Gerwani at those moments when Mother Pertiwi Was Late in
Her Pregnancy recalled her mother the late Ma Legimah who used
to purvey fried cassava snacks in front of the Chinese temple at the
corner of the barracks city's town square; well granted Iin wasn't a
good daughter to the person who had borne and nursed her, she rarely
remembered her generous mother Ma Legimah the wife of the KNIL
corporal; it wasn't because she was ashamed to have a mother who
was just a peasant woman, but because for some reason her own
womb within herself hardly mattered to her; maybe because she was
the younger sister of a twin older brother, so the elements of her
body were largely dominated by the masculine capitalist imperialist or maybe because her womb had been so poisoned by NEFIS soldiers her maidenhood had been wrenched from her so disgustingly
that her womb had dropped dead and what remained was a body
that only appeared to have a womb and breasts but in fact had turned
into a mattress that's soft sure but lifeless, fit only to be bought and
sold as long as it doesn't smell yet and isn't all spotted with bed-
wetting stains so all that's left to do is rip it open and take out the
stuffing, just a mattress that needs to be taken outdoors regularly
every week or few days and beaten with a cane after it's been aired
in the sun. A woman really needs some sort of Wall of China so as
not to get battered open by a gang of thugs, but while the worthy
Gerwani officials knew about this line of thinking, they still posted
women to defensive positions where spontaneous movement was
difficult. On the contrary! Tiwi and all the other Gerwani were created in order to aggressively attack assault and advance!

Still one day suddenly there was a great commotion among the *kamerads* from Indonesia who had just heard on the rebel radio that a Revolutionary Council had risen up in Jakarta, and that at last Mother Pertiwi had delivered a new baby consisting of the revolutionary forces that had in fact already taken control of all of Jakarta, Central Java, and East Java, and that dozens of reactionary generals had been hanged or thrown into the sea and that Bung Karno had brilliantly demonstrated his abilities as Great Leader of the Revolution and Highest Commander of the Armed Forces, and was now setting policy from Halim Air Field, and that the first loads of weapons had been put to the best and most efficient use possible, and that the entire populace was standing behind Bung Karno, thanks to the first gun shipments from Beijing and so forth and so on and so on and so forth. But on the third day after the announcement of the Revolutionary Council's formation, her *kamerad* fellows had all scattered who knows where, and *Kamerad* Tiwi, the only female member of the delegation, was left all alone. So making use of the most opportune facilities, without panicking, Miss Tiwi went by train to Guangzhou then to Kowloon and was able thanks to her Republic of Indonesia diplomatic passport to cross to Hong Kong, to look for the worthy former bald youth with the wooden rifle whose secret address she had learned. Their meeting after so many years' separation and because of the new situation wasn't all that warm, but because Pertiwi had come up and straightaway hugged and kissed Him, the atmosphere could still be pronounced pretty secure, even though they knew that the moment had now come that Deputy Prime Minister Soebandrio had predicted in January a year earlier, that in the year 1965 it would become clear how friends in the revolutionary struggle could become foes, concretely it was quite possible that the former half-lovers, half-commercial partners had started to draw lines among those who were friends and those who were foes; but that didn't worry Auntie Wi because her everyday experience had taught her that any man, whether friend or foe, always turned into a friend if he felt the softness of a woman's body; thus she embarked on that very procedure and at that very moment with the highly placed intelligence officer whose hair now shone luxuriantly with the help of the Hong Kong Night brand, with the end result that they spent a number of *Hong Kong Nights* and for that matter *Hong Kong Days* in ways that were not in the least bit revolutionary since they have been practiced since the days when Adam's rib turned into a cute and comely curvaceous attractive creature, even though in a style yet undiscovered by the *old established forces* generation, who are worse than the liberal bourgeois.

Still what mattered most, out of that dialectic of thesis and antithesis of friend and foe half-romantic half-commercial, was that Auntie Wi succeeded in obtaining the synthesis of three fake diplomatic passports along with of course three types of passport photos, to choose among according to the situation, in exchange for Mr. Former Wooden Rifle getting a *check* worth about one sack of Dutch silver coins like what sank in the boat of that former KNIL corporal and *heiho* who was sent on assignment from Halmahera long before, a sum that didn't amount to so much as *een rimpel in de ocean* or a little ripple on the surface of the ocean, as the Great Leader of the Revolution and the one Revolution expert in all of Nusantara said about the victims at the Crocodile Hole and Cakrabirawa; but Auntie Wi was convinced that even though she was out all that private capital that she had gathered painstakingly over so many years filled with neighborhood lending societies cabinets getting named and dismissed and Army Chiefs of Staff and a great inflation in the number of political parties, MPRS and DPRGR sessions and all kinds of resolutions, nevertheless Auntie Wi still felt herself in possession of a source of capital she could rely upon at all times, namely a biological capital as soft and sweet as fried cassava snacks with perfect vital statistics for launching her own personal revolution, in accordance with the speech of the President Commander-in-Chief Great Leader of the Revolution Mandatee of the MPRS on August 17, 1965, entitled

"Reach for the Stars in the Sky." Thus calmly and self-possessed although very homesick and anxiously asking herself what the fate of her beloved artist in Yogyakarta might be, the man she had been obliged to leave behind in a rush because she had been called to Jakarta for an important duty, Auntie Wi flew to Singapore to have a careful thorough consultation about the possibility of having plastic surgery that would meet her many and difficult demands, at a famous plastic surgery clinic; thus the secret operation deemed possible decided and done a great success, took place on March 11, 1966, the exact date of Supersemar Day. Thus Iin Sulinda Pertiwi, child of the former KNIL corporal and *heiho* and the fried-cassava-snack seller from in front of the Chinese temple at the corner of the Magelang town square, came out of that plastic clinic ready and right as Madame Angelin Ruth Portier born to Meester Cornelis, son of father Mijnheer Willem Pieter Portier and mother Pailah Kromodimejo of Prontakan in Magelang, alias *Madame* Charlotte Eugenie, youngest daughter of father François de Xavier Pierre Charles Baron du Bois de la Montagne (calling herself the widow Nussy de Proguelêaux) and mother Wang Ching Mei, Border Alley Semarang, alias Tukinah Senik (calling herself the widow Madame Nusa Musbida) of father Colonel Yamashita and Ma Basket, from Cokrodiningratan in Yogyakarta; everything matched or came pretty close amazingly enough to the passport photos in the three passports conjured up by the former bald youth with the wooden rifle who was posted to Hong Kong; and really truly it was really amazing, since the Day of March 11, 1966, Tiwi's face had metamorphosed to become completely different, formerly she had been a little cutie from Central Java's Tidar Progo and Elo region, but now there was a bit of the China miss or those special Eurasian sorts of spices, so you might guess she was a Macao girl with a bit of Portuguese mixed in, or maybe French mixed with Japanese, but you wouldn't be wrong to think of her as a *cokri* (chick) or *perokum lemot paten bintrok bohay* (a beautiful gorgeous sexy babe) of Jakarta's ritzy Menteng quarter, a melding of chromosomal

DNA of Bombay, Morocco, Lisbon, Amsterdam, Shanghai, Priangan, Samosir, and Kawanua; a professional note: she's the owner and special director of the Global Joy Corporation with all its conglomerate arms trunks and tentacles that can provide cover for pretty much anything, especially in the tourism field. So there you have *Madame* Nussy de Proguelêaux, a very skilled devotee of foreign investment who without fear of suspicion or arrest could return via Jakarta's Halim Airport or Yogyakarta's Adisucipto into the heart of the Republic of Indonesia's Revolution-era capital and into the aristocratic compounds near the Sultan's palace, to look for the painter for whom her heart longed; with the pretext that she was bringing a letter and package, a present from his grandfather in Singaraja for him. But after asking here and there great was her surprise and shock when she heard from the Neighborhood Head that her beloved painter's safety had been assured by the authorities, he had entered Wirogunan prison and people say his safety had been further assured in the prison on Kambangan Island, and causing her still greater *shock,* the Neighborhood Head told her sorrowfully that the older lady who was beautiful dignified and calm had died after she had gotten a letter from her son saying that Rohadi was to be transported the next day along with ten thousand other political prisoners to an island a long way from Java. According to the Neighborhood Head, it was really strange Rohadi was a young painter who was friendly and polite and well liked by people in the neighborhood who would have expected who would have suspected it turned out there was a snake in the sheets, poison in the drinks, because only later did intelligence in Yogyakarta discover he had a special secret assignment from Lekra to prepare for the failed Revolutionary Councils; as an agent who received secret instructions from a cadre in fact she was his girlfriend as well a woman of the Gerwani Central Management and Lekra who in the preparations for Mother Pertiwi Is Late in Her Pregnancy had constantly paid him calls and stayed over at his house for that matter; according to Intelligence, her name was Pertiwi, and the neighborhood youths had been suspicious about her for a long time but they hadn't done anything to her yet because they didn't have enough evidence, till all their rotten secrets were exposed when a platoon from the Extraordinary Military Tribunal screening and prosecuting team from Jakarta came having in their possession a list of all the big shots in Gerwani and Lekra; so please Madam, as a foreign tourist who of course doesn't know about the great tragedy that swept over the Indonesian people in the years '65 and '66, for your own good leave here quick as you can and just make up some fake story about Rohadi for his grandfather in Singaraja who apparently still doesn't know who his grandson was and where he is now, so the old man won't get a shock and his heart stop; but as a matter of fact it would be a smart move, Madam, since of course you don't know and have nothing to do with the Revolutionary Council coup business in Yogyakarta that made victims of two high commanders and a great many people whether guilty or innocent, well that's what our people are like, Madam, we look quiet peaceful cool and calm but suddenly all at once erupt like Mt. Merapi, then everything gets smashed without rhyme or reason; thus it would be best Madam if you made as though you had never come around to look in on the painter's house and we'll keep quiet in a thousand languages too, because of course Madam as a tourist you don't know the ins-and-outs and twists-and-turns of the G-30S tragedy which Bung Karno called Gestok but he was wrong; Gestok sounds like the Armed Forces started the movement on the morning of October 1, but what happened only came after the September 30 Movement; and that to this day we're still in the process of cleaning up sorting out who's a friend who's a foe, who's Lekra and who's Pancasila, anyway we wish you a safe trip and thanks for your concern Miss . . . Miss . . . well I'm sorry I don't know how to pronounce your name.

A thousand thanks, too, kind lady, for your contribution to our neighborhood treasury; maybe we'll use it to build a more representative guardhouse in the interests of security and order, but the neighborhood will have to take this up for discussion; the problem is that the young guys want a net and volleyball and a communal guitar because they say a guitar is more important than a guard post; and as far as that goes I myself personally, not as the Neighborhood Head, I agree completely, because you know a guitar is more practical and clearly cheaper and furthermore you can use it to provide mental and spiritual support and generate some enthusiasm among the young guys doing watchmen's rounds at night; and gee it really is too bad Rohadi got tripped up by that Lekra woman's cajoling, actually he was a nice guy and he always gave the guys "sweetshot" tea, hot thick and sweet, when they passed by his house on their rounds; and it was too bad for his poor mother who loved him so much she came to Yogya to look for her son, well it's not surprising here she was a widow with only the one child and he was so nice; oh it's tragic really tragic he got hooked on that Gerwani girl she was pretty for sure but clearly older than he was and it's like it was reincarnation the law of karma for spiders the way they eat the male after they've sorry you know uh done it together, sorry but anyway that was always the way, those were the communists' tactics; exactly like Goddess Durga the way sometimes she takes on a beautiful woman's appearance with Lady Umayi's looks but it turns out she's going to drag her victim to Corpstenchfield to eat him raw; well pretty women really are very dangerous, oh I'm sorry, I'm sorry, I'm really sorry, I didn't mean to suggest anything about you, Madam, you're certainly not Goddess Durga, of course you don't know who Goddess Durga is Madam, and of course as a tourist you don't have any connection to all this, but it's best it's wiser for you never to look for the young Balinese painter's house again, because you know yourself, Madam, once someone's under suspicion they're as good as found guilty already, so better to be careful; once again thank you for your contribution to the neighborhood's community chest; and have a good trip home to your own country, which is it oh yes France, Javanese call it Parangakik, Parang means coral in the ocean, while akik is a precious stone, so your country must be very beautiful like a jewel in the middle of the sea, a voar okay a voar,[1] I still remember a few words of Parangakik from my MULO[2] days, a voar and bong bong voyaaasye! Hahahaaa yes mersi biyèn, mersi biyèn.[3]

Shattered shredded, Tiwi Nussy's heart was the heart of a woman going on forty or so okay no longer young but didn't she still have the right to love and be loved, didn't she have the right to embrace and kiss a young man who was ideal who was an almost perfect man for her even if only subjectively and this Mr. Right was 10 years her junior, but isn't it true that all love is subjective? And now it was she yes it was Nussy it was Tiwi who had become the direct cause of her idol's destruction who although he was ten years her junior responded to the beating of her heart; her dear Idol who always appears in the evening behind the window curtained with Coromandel velvet edged in Kashmiri lace, then bows elegantly gripping flowers in his right hand and in his left a hat that dances to the side, then approaches her bed with the steps of a *troubadour perfect d'amour*,[4] then kisses her; oh why did Mother Pertiwi have to get pregnant again, was it true like what the Neighborhood Head said a bit ago that Iin Linda Pertiwi was in reality the great Durga who had once been the beautiful Lady Umayi but because she was cursed by the likes of Lord Guru turned into this sort of female monster, and even had the heart to murder a young lover who was refined and noble of mind, even though not on purpose, but what meaning does on purpose or not on purpose have in this life; and is it true that every revolution swallows up its own children; or is all of this sim-

---

1. Till we meet again.
2. SMTP [Sekolah Menengah Teknik Pertama=Junior Technical Middle School] in the Dutch Indies period.
3. Safe trip, thank you.
4. A perfect singer of love songs.

ply *een rimpel in de oceaan* like the Great Leader of the Revolution commented about the murder of eight Armed Forces men at the Crocodile Hole but eight times eighty thousand ordinary folks got slaughtered poor things who didn't know to do anything except just do what everybody was doing because they were ignorant but still they weren't in the wrong like Rohadi himself, with the result that Nussy no longer had a handsome hero laddie Rohadi.

Thus she wept she agonized and everything seemed futile in the mind and guts of this woman filled with the drama of experiences she had never expected and never requested, who was super rich pretty attractive with a Eurasian's perfect features but it was all a lie with three passports and three kinds of passport photos and a fake appearance the work of a plastic surgery clinic, indeed a Eurasian of the highest status precisely because she had lost her identity and her true self and true form, she had become a not-self, the result of sophisticated technological surgery and savings accounts in foreign banks outside her homeland which while overflowing yet were the results of lobbying and fishing in the turbid water of post-independence crisis political intrigue; rich in material things and poor in love, empty in her own being, her identity lost; a spectacular career woman like an astronaut in space but paralyzed dependent on a cable that could break at any moment or not keep the oxygen flowing or the electric current, without solid ground to assure her steps; she was no longer Iin Sulinda Pertiwi, but who knows was she Angelin Ruth or Charlotte Eugenie or Tukinah Senik, what was clear was that she was none of the three but then again no longer the sweetheart of the Microphone of 56 East Pegangsaan Street who had been gone for a long time now never turned up anymore to entertain her and give her strength, because even the Proclamation house had been destroyed leveled to the ground; and it would be just as obvious and a matter of course if the esteemed Microphone didn't even know her anymore and would fail to recognize Madam Investor in big tourism projects and anything else she got her hands on, a person

without a homeland who went on the Concorde from Paris to New
York and had breakfast in Tokyo then did some lobbying in Paris,
London, and Helsinki then *lunch* in Rio de Janeiro to spend the night
dancing in a Hong Kong disco and sleep with a gigolo in Puerto Rico
and suddenly turns up passing through the VIP gate at Halim Airport then Cengkareng, well how could the dear Microphone recognize her with this super-Eurasian multiracial cosmopolitan face; with
clothes from Christian Dior, with bags from Hermès, smoking
Camels and staying at the Hilton, and lobbying in her private room
a marshal a general an admiral and big weapons merchants' agents
sent by Khassogi and Vietnamese intelligence personnel and the gold-
smuggling bosses from Capetown and ivory from Nairobi and
cocaine from Colombia and tourist business conglomerates from
Bangkok who have a lot to do with the trade in women both low
class and high; well really you can understand why her eminent friend
the dear Microphone rarely visited her after the Roundtable Conference and stopped visiting altogether once West Irian returned to
the arms of the Homeland, this despite the fact that Iin was now a
whole lot prettier and more highly skilled than she had been when
she was a laundrywoman, so in principle she brought more glory to
her nation because she could hold her own among representatives
of the world of *beauty queens* and *mannequins* from advanced countries, she didn't feel intimidated but on the contrary walked self-
confidently with her head up swaying gracefully in the reception halls
and lobbies of national ceremonies and high business, bending elegantly as though she were floating above a marble floor among the
giant crystal flower bouquets and the glow of the lights, in her evening
clothes, creations and handiwork of the fingers of the god Yves St.
Laurent *himself,* bared-back-and-breast gowns that swelled up about
her svelte slim slender form, slit on the side to her calf to her thigh
in a very civic-minded fashion with those matching cheeks inviting
slaps, with a pair of soft fruits bulging on her chest, as though feck-
lessly forgetting it's forbidden to goad guys and instead gesturing

sweetly suggesting sensuous oblivion but still tauntingly, which makes people dazed dreamy distended distracted desirous curiously supposing just supposing oh wouldn't it be . . . oh, how could her friend the Microphone of 56 East Pegangsaan Street recognize her again and kiss her and entice her to speak, yes, go ahead and speak a few words my dear Iin, if even her name card says Angelin Ruth Charlotte Eugenie?

So Angeline binti Wang Ching Mei was caught short and startled early one morning one month of August, it was as if a faint voice from far away was calling her moaning: Iin, Iin! Say who could it be that still knows her real name is Iin, who . . . who . . . maybe Rohadi on X Island? How could that be, to Rohadi she was never Iin but Pertiwi. Nevertheless through her secretary who was a tough old bird but knew the addresses of all the Mafia and Yakuza and Triad[5] guys who had been trying all morning to get notes to her about meeting with several big honcho cocaine importers from Miami Florida who were interested in buying one lot of marijuana from Aceh, *Madame* Nussy rudely wrathfully ordered the damned old secretary to get a *VIP-class ticket* ready at once with the best *schedule* to Denpasar Bali with connections to X Island, and that the cocaine matter could be put off for now; or if they wanted it okay at the price that had been sent a week earlier using a secret code through the participating Mafia networks; and if they didn't want to okay fine, *Madame* Nussy de Proguelêaux didn't need those lecherous larcenists' pitiful dollars, and that she *Punyo* Nusamusbida knew only about *fair business* unstained by filth and corruption. Thus by means of secret channels and concealed connections known only to a certain number of *very important* people, Mrs. Nusamusbida arrived (in a letter of assignment she was named Ad Hoc Inspector seconded to the Concinbod

---

5. Mafia=bandit gangs originally from Sicily; Yakuza=bandit gangs in Japan; Triad=bandit gangs in Hong Kong.

[Consolidated Central Intelligence Body] Mrs. Inspector reached Z, went on to the subdistrict office of Y on X Island; and at the Commando Headquarters she asked straightaway if there was a political prisoner named Rohadi from Bali but who used to live in Yogya; that's right he was an artist but not necessarily Lekra, and where's his unit; is he in the Hope Triumphant unit or the Joyful Labor unit or Happiness to Follow unit or maybe in the one crammed full of pinko intellectuals from HIS, CGMI, IPPI,[6] Lekra and famous poets and novelists in the Development's Dawning Spirit unit?

It turned out there was indeed someone, precisely like the person our esteemed Mrs. Nusamusbida from Concinbod was asking about, but we're very sorry Madam, for about a year he'd been showing abnormal symptoms it's quite sad; maybe because of *stress* maybe because he was still stuck in the poison of Marxist teachings, maybe because he missed his wife but very possibly too it was just because he'd gotten tropical malarial mosquito bites, in short Madam, our friend Rohadi who's famous for being good at painting and playing the guitar disappeared a few days ago running off into the jungles of this island, and we only just found him early this morning, Ma'am, south of here; maybe he wanted to run to the South Coast, Ma'am, but that would be impossible a waste because he'd have to cross the wild forests full of very vicious beasts and where the original inhabitants of this island live and they're still cannibals; so that's the way it is Ma'am, strange but true Ma'am, turns out they found him about one day's journey on foot, Ma'am, but it's really a shame the ants and cockroaches had already gotten him, he didn't have a head, it was horrible Ma'am, but an unfortunate incident like this even though it's tragic still it's good too Ma'am, it's very useful for us, as an example for the other guys who are still thinking about try-

---

6. Academics', university students', and schoolchildren's communist organizations.

ing to escape Ma'am, from the prison camp which actually is Pancasila humanitarian, but what can you do Ma'am, there's no way communist prisoners are going to be given lodgings like in Puncak with millionaires' bungalows and luxury, isn't that right Madam, that's not why we've spent so many billion rupiah developing X Island; but if you like, Mrs. Musbida from Concinbod, you might be so good as to inform Rohadi's mother, if she's still alive or his grandmother or uncle if they're still living and where because certainly an agency like Concinbod knows everyone's address who was implicated as far as their kin to the second degree and below and to the side including the parents-in-law and other in-laws, so that at the very least his mother or grandmother or brothers and sisters know, that Rohadi is calm and at peace resting in the embrace of the All-Beneficent and All-Forgiving Lord, even though he was a Lekra communist; and one more request if you would Mrs. Musbida, this really matters Ma'am, please be sure to report and propose to the Central Administration Ma'am that they further develop their policy toward the 10,000 political prisoners here Ma'am; sorry about this Ma'am, but here are these guys who haven't seen a woman in seven or eight years, really Ma'am, so in the name of the Just and Civilized Humanitarian Principle among the Five Principles of the Nation they should start a *crash program* to send as many whores from Jakarta as possible transport them here to X Island, so that they can be legally married according to their respective religious affiliations to these men who for so many years haven't so much as seen what a woman looks like, sorry Ma'am that's just how it is, if only for the sake of *security* so they don't get rough and unruly, wild like a starving lion; it matters Ma'am, because this is sure to compromise the image of the Country and Nation; this way we can kill two birds with one stone we can reduce the number of whores in Java's cities that are getting more and more crowded and the newspapers say keep getting more degenerate and hard to control Ma'am; furthermore point number 2 is with regard to the division of profits in an outfit such as ours, with 10,000 unpaid workers, there's a big incentive Ma'am; isn't it the case that the matter of the division of profits should be considered in a comparative fashion as a percentage-based portion of the profits that's fairer and corresponds to the effort of all productive components; except of course for the labor factor which is free, Madam, and so forth and so on and so on and so forth, Madam, isn't that right, Madam, really Ma'am, forgive me for all this Ma'am.

Okay, it's easy to forgive them because they're just taking orders, but how could Nussy forgive herself for her exploits that had caused a cherished young artist to be sentenced to death when he had done nothing wrong? Well maybe he is happily reunited with his mother who was elegant and whose beauty appeared just the same as when she was young even though she was already a grandmother; thus all of a sudden worthy Iin in the inner recesses of *Madame* Nussy de Proguelêaux's heart cried and moaned; she had a mother who she remembered from her childhood getting up early every morning and sitting in front of that Chinese temple to sell fried cassava snacks; Iin knew about that because sometimes if she got up too early she'd whine and whimper so her mother would take her along to that corner of the town square, she'd squat beside her mother who was busy serving the devotees of fried cassava snacks; then they'd go home passing by the Muslim quarter and the Mosque and at the corner of the bridge over the canal from the Regent's Office wow was it ever yummy she could buy a banana leaf packet of stewed jackfruit and rice; maybe with a thin strip of chicken maybe with just a quarter of an egg, because yummy things are expensive for a woman who only sells fried cassava snacks; and Dad was only a KNIL corporal for that matter who often had to treat his soldier buddies to food, because he often got treated to beer himself; and anyway that's what life was like for barracks soldiers in the age of steam engine locomotives in Magelang that still puff-pant-ding-ding-choooo-choo went ploughing across Chinatown Street crowded with people, as though they thought of themselves as soldiers in the East

India Company's army with tanks out in front or drummers but loony
drummers with loony bells ding-ding-ding-hey-get-out-of-the-way-
or-you'll-end-up-flat-as-a-dime; oh why did Iin never think about her
late mother anymore the fried-cassava-snack seller who bore her and
nursed her carried her on her hip bought her rich yummy stewed
jackfruit and rice with a quarter of a salted egg? Iin wept Linda
moaned Tiwi was wracked with homesickness oh could life be done
over again like those Hindus believe, so that our *Madame* rich-but-
wretched could get free of the excesses entangling disorienting and
disagreeable turning her into Durga the source of other people's ruin,
rewarding her by taking away her lover whom she had so recently
embraced-imbibed? Yet a little while later these feelings of regret and
weakness gave way in turn to a violent explosion of her heart as she
went into a rage, went amok went berserk without measure; cursing
uncontrollably spitting filthy insulting words about the rottenness of
men, about what pigs all those egotistical cronies and old boys are
who only know how to use people and look out for themselves with
no sense of justice or *fair play;* that they really aren't businessmen but
reckless speculators who ride their power like a steamroller, terror-
izing anyone they think threatens to compete with them; and that
politics is dirty and all those ideologies whether communist who cares
liberal who cares and the other isms are nonsense and messy-big-talk
leaky-hole-stopping rags for half-baked minds; and Miss Bi screamed
hysterically and drove out all the devils nesting in her chest and all
the gall of frustration concealed for years and years since she had gotten NEFISed by those bullying guys who are all the same everywhere,
exactly the same, six of one a half dozen of the other.

But one afternoon baked by the hot sun, making poor workers
sweat in Abu Dhabi of the United Arab Emirates, *Madame* Nussy
was enjoying a bubble bath fragrant like the tropicana clouds in the
sky, in a bathroom tiled with genuine Italian marble and a toilet and
bidet of Chinese jade and faucets of 20 carat gold, with crystal mir-

rors as big as Rembrandt's *Nachtwacht*[7] in Amsterdam, so that everything showed in all natural nakedness like at a *striptease* theatre, and
while she was comfortably luxuriating in the fragrant bubble clouds
that enveloped rubbed stroked her nakedness, then again yes once
again she heard a voice very faintly: Iin, Iin, Iin! It called worryingly
whimpering wanting help, who but who on earth could it be that
knew her old nickname Iin? All at once Miss Bi jumped up and jumped
out naked but for bubbles and bathwater and picked up the phone
nearby, called her decrepit old secretary and ordered her to line up
a *VIP-class ticket* to Jakarta to charter a Boeing 737 if necessary, straight
to Yogya or Solo with orders for a special *super-de-luxe* jeep to meet
her for a possible trip to the interior in the western region. So off she
flew *Madame* Nussy de Proguelêaux with all those suitcases and bags
all of them from Hermès Paris; once again she arrived at Soekarno-
Hatta International Airport without needing to show a passport or
visa, got into a BMW parked beneath the plane, went to another plane
chartered from Prambanan Shuttle Air Service (another one of the
dozens of branch trunk tentacle businesses she owned) and off she
flew once again *Madame* Nussy accompanied only by her decrepit
secretary but she knows all the ins-and-outs of the Mafia, Yakuza
and Triad, to Adisucipto field in Yogya where a *super-de-luxe* jeep was
already waiting for her near the plane, complete with a diminutive
but feisty lady tour guide, a real Srikandi, doubling as the driver, then
passed through the VIP gate on to the Imperial Hotel, to speed on
once she had bathed and eaten up into the hills she was intent upon
reaching; without attendant other than the polite refined retiring
sweet little driver but a Roban devil behind the wheel, speeding like
they were on a racecourse to the address it made good sense for them
to be going to, namely Iin's twin older brother Brother Brojol's vil-

---

7. A famous painting: *The Nightwatch.*

lage, who knows how life has treated him after so many dozen years without meeting up with or writing him.

But how great was her shock how great was the blow, all Iin found oh God oh God had Iin gotten lost or forgotten where her twin older brother lived? No! They asked a village headman, a snack stall owner, a farmer by a field, again they asked a goatherd by the side of the road, a peasant woman carrying firewood on her back who was passing by, they all said that's right, yes there that's right yea let's see over there, right, here near here yes the village and her brother Pa Brojol's houseyard would be right here, because back in the time of taking unilateral action against village devils, Tiwi had gone down to the masses in the area and had a chance to spend half a day with her brother who still didn't want to join up with the Indonesian Peasants' Front, one of the pillars of the Revolution; well clearly it should have been there but *mon Dieu,*[8] what did she see? The whole valley had been dug up that used to be so fertile with green gold rice fields mirroring the sky, with villages like heavenly islands almost always billowing with the melodious sounds of a gamelan orchestra soothing hearts and making people feel content, with the twisting turning curling curving snaking ribboning rivers that sometimes flashed silver the radiance of the fortune-bearing clouds, sometimes looked like the dark flow of melted coconut sugar and sticky rice, but now well now *mijn God,*[9] the whole valley had been turned upside down by hundreds of bulldozers and thousands of dump trucks so the landscape looked like a tin mine or the surface of the moon, what the hell is this, and where's Brother Brojol? *Madame* Nussy wandered around for a long time with her hands in her pockets with her arms crossed on her chest with her hands on her hips filled with a rainbow of questions and darkest puzzles, what's going on down there

8. My God.
9. My God.

in that valley; but all of a sudden with a jolt with a start eyes agape mouth ajar running her fingers through her hair, then standing with her hands on her hips she got enraged and swore: Shithead!—so loud the startled driver thought she was the one getting cussed out, but clearly that wasn't it because *Madame* Nussy had her back turned to the jeep, where the driver was sitting trying to have a nap, at least to close her eyes for a bit because she was tired from driving all this way. Shithead! And the shithead had to be *Madame* Nussy de Proguelêaux herself who suddenly looked like she had been struck by lightning to her brain and her memory realizing that this very valley which had been so prosperous pretty beautiful and now had been torn up and turned upside down by so many hundreds of bull-dozers and so many thousands of dump trucks that's right this very valley was the location of the project which she had signed the con-tract for with her gold Cartier pen a year ago, going in with several in-country conglomerates, backed up by the World Bank, the Asian Development Bank plus a little more funding from private banks in the USA and Hong Kong and Singapore; with managing contractors from Japan, Australia, under the authority of an international con-sortium; with official board members from the Government and some bigwigs from the mass media both state-owned and private to influence *public opinion,* rounded out by all those dozens of psychol-ogists, sociologists, anthropologists, geologists, and civil engineers and water and electricity technicians; plus famous names from the world of art and culture, representatives from the palaces full of ven-erable traditions and people's folk arts associations; and many more consultants and analysts from the brainy university world as well as the Cultural Research Centers, consultants from the Center for Strategic and International Research and the Think Tank Indonesia in the XXIst Century; and of course from Armed Forces and Intelli-gence Bureau circles in an integral and comprehensive manner, thus both very professionally and also democratically; all of them coor-dinated and combined to build a giant superproject in a stunning-

striking-tourism-studytour framework with 17 main aims, and 8 special program tracks on a lot of 1945 hectares following five suitabil-
ity studies by the above teams who declared by acclamation that:
in the interests of development and increasing productivity values,
acceleration modernization and mobilization of the population, in
the valley we'll just call Brother Brojol's Valley hands-in-the-cookie-
jar magic financing would make it possible to put up a sort of Disneyland only featuring high points of indigenous culture from the
whole archipelago complete with 1945 five-star hotels and motels
including restaurants, discos (and it's still being kept secret *sex-shops*)
17 banks plus 8 casinos and a world-map-in-miniature garden with
each country's and continent's attractions and specialties on a scale
that has been shown to work well at Madurodam in the Netherlands,
hey it's really fantastic; of course all of this will be in an attractive
composite architectural style and layout with artificial lakes, artificial
basins and dams, artificial rivers streams and canals, gardens for leisure
and romance both artificial and natural, with facilities for golf, ten-
nis, water skiing, kite racing, car racing, and formula this and that
motorcycles, *holidays on ice,* in a word the biggest in all of Asia and
the Pacific; but don't forget about the study center concept, with a
supercolossal museum complete with panoramas and dioramas of
the guerrilla struggle against the Dutch on a 1:10 scale that displays
all the battles that took place during the wars for independence, starting from the resistance of the sultans of Aceh, Ternate, and Bugis,
and the Banda chiefs, the kings of Mataram, Bali, Banten, and others in the VOC Dutch East Indies period (except of course the Indonesian Communist Party's strikes and uprisings in the Dutch East Indies
period) up to the regaining of West Irian; indeed this is very much
needed for the sake of education and for passing on the legacy of
our ancestors' values; but in the name of the 21st century there will
also be pictures, schemas, and dioramas about Indonesian astronauts'
journeys to the moon and combined transmigration projects from
shabby big-city neighborhoods to the planet Mars; and a kind of wax

museum like *Madame* Tussaud's in London, where all the figures will
be of guerrilla leaders but also of Indonesian nationals who are potential Nobel Prize winners in physics, chemistry, economics, and not
to forget gastronomy given the honor recorded in the *Guinness Book
of World Records* in the form of a cake picturing the entire archipelago on a scale of 1:500, really, in short the whole thing will be colos-
sal and fabulous, in line with the name of our homeland: Glorious
Indonesia.

So there you have it the pride-of-place project that *Madame* Nussy
had signed off on; only bad luck: one mistake she had made, she had
forgotten to ask or to look to see on a really detailed map put out by
the US Army where the project was to be located; she only knew
that it was on Java but at the time she was really careless reckless
just leave it up to them whatever, absent-minded inattentive about
checking personally herself where it was going to be operational-
ized; no surprise since at the time *Madame* was busy with all the ins-
and-outs twists-and-turns of lobbying and diplomacy concerning
weapons supplies for all sides in Lebanon, Iran, and Iraq, the San-
dinistas and the Contras too and of course Cambodia, so that really
*mon Dieu mijn God,* she forgot, plain forgot that there was still this
guy called Brojol and he was her older twin brother; who unexpectedly unintentionally "here's the rap Muslim cap" was just the
one who got hurt got steamrollered got tractored got dumptrucked,
oh dear oh no "cassava snack felt like a smack," poor Iin Linda Pertiwi Punyo Nusamusbida was logey limp really devastated; it was
horrifying, really horrifying because she had once heard at a one-
day seminar that the fates of twins are very closely bound up
together, in the sense that they pull on each other in a single vibra-
tion a single sentiment or even take opposite paths in their aspirations and ends, but still they aren't free of each other; as a matter of
fact all this time she hadn't taken the opportunity to ask an expert,
and now she felt the effects of this error and carelessness on her part,
that is she had forgotten to ask the professionals, whether Brojol and

Iin were twins from a single egg or from two eggs, now they say
this really matters; it's very different from cassava-snack rounds that
you can fry together or separately, so don't let it happen that this
pride-of-place project turn out to be the weapon that does its master in, oh man it's horrifying frightening worrying the heart of this
Srikandi who had never once felt frightened or worried before.

She was in such a daze this career woman contractor sitting on
the ground in complete confusion that she didn't realize dozens of
kids were swarming around her, watching in amazement and curiosity this modern creature who for sure came from Jakarta, because
her slacks and blouse and dark glasses and shoes were really neat
weird crazy, the kids thought she looked like a clown but a really
rich one, because her jeep was shiny and sparkled with a new coat
of wax with silver-rimmed wheels and the tires were strange really
wide ones; and then there was the driver asleep in the seat, maybe
she was a woman but she didn't have breasts like their mothers and
sisters but her silk blouse glittered white it was so clean there was
no way you could get anything like that in a village and a lot of
bracelets and what about all those rings, all kinds of them and her
mouth with shiny red lipstick and those sunglasses are something
with gold frames and a hat God like a general's; meanwhile inside
the jeep the kids could see big thermoses and one was open and inside
it was real ice cream the color of river mud and yellow like bamboo
but it must have been delicious tasting, and different kinds of cakes
all wrapped up, yeah for sure for sure this was a rich tourist lady. Suddenly from the rear emerged a loud rough sound from a mustachioed
mouth like a snake-charmer's, a man passing by yelling at the children to get away from that jeep, "Hey get out of there, acting like the
village kids you are, shame on you, what have you never seen a car
before, and you've never seen a woman, like you're looking at a per-
forming monkey, it's an outrage; come on, get out, you're a disgrace
to your parents!" And many other such reproaches. Thus the kids ran
scurrying away from the car and *Madame* Nussy and her driver who

was probably a woman, only to come back again like flies whose ritual is indeed to get chased away so they can come back again.

The man approached and asked personably of the woman who did he thought look like a clown the way she was dressed but a very rich clown; maybe this was a tourist from America who had gotten lost, and although he hesitated doubting whether he'd be able to communicate with her in his very backwoods-sounding Indonesian, still he screwed up his courage to help her should it turn out she needed help; because who knows, in this day and age when people realize tourism's many enchantments people have to realize too that tourists have money and you need to clean them out of as much as possible; but luckily once he had begun the conversation with, hello Madam, sori ai em departemen informesiyen hir in kelurahan, pelis ai help yu ai ken du wot for yu? it turned out the esteemed lady could speak Indonesian although her accent made her speak through her nose, still it was clear, so she was looking for a guy whose name was *Mesieur* Brojol from such-and-such village; oh for goodness sake all you're looking for is Brojol, sure I know him, everybody knows old Brojol; a good guy but plain-talking and he knows what he wants, he was the son of a *heiho;* hey who do you suppose this woman is, does Brojol have foreign backing and connections? Hey this is a risky business, but then again you could get lucky; so okay let's just let her think I'm an official in the Department of Information around here, but this is one strange kind of a woman, how come she can speak Indonesian so well even if it is through her nose? But a long straight nose well that's what it's for to show off when you speak; say watch it this could be old Brojol's younger sister but hey she doesn't look anything like him; ha ha ha so even that Brojol has something going on on the side, the bastard, but no way some woman this rich and a foreigner to boot is going to fall for dumb old Brojol. It's true Pa Brojol often talked about having some twin sister in Jakarta, but then Pa Brojol himself didn't know where she had gotten to, he always says she's sure to come back on Idul Fitri but every Idul Fitri we wait to see who's going to say she's Pa Brojol's twin sister and she never turns up; he also says maybe she got killed by the Dutch or the Communist Party or who knows who because he never gets any letters from her or the tiniest bit of news, so once he even put on a ceremony for the soul of the sister he said had disappeared, it was sad of course but still they were sure to meet up again in heaven along with their father and mother, said dumb old Brojol: yes Ma'am, Pa Brojol is actually a newcomer to our village, his father was from way out in Kebumen Bagelen, his mother from Parakan Candiroto, but funny it seemed like right away he felt at home living with his widowed mother-in-law in our village well our former village, since now our village has gotten buried underneath those tractors and trucks good Lord is the whole place ever a mess; but I'm terribly sorry Madam but might I ask, who you are actually, are you his niece? Because, or so thought the worthy Department of Information officer, she clearly wasn't that twin sister of his, since Madam's complexion is the pale yellow of young langsat fruit whereas Pa Brojol's is as dark as the heart of a hardwood tree; but of course nothing's certain since Pa Brojol is a newcomer to the village and not a single person in the village has ever seen that twin sister of his; if Madam is so inclined, I'll take you along to Pa Brojol's place but it's like this Madam, it's really too bad about Pa Brojol, well you'll see for yourself, it's too bad about everything around here, it's rough Madam, let's go ahead and go; but you'll have to leave your jeep here Madam, is that all right? Oh oh fine fine, Ms. Driver can watch it here; hey kids don't do anything stupid any of you, this is a minister's car from Jakarta, watch out if any of you brats scratch it up with your fingernails you'll end up in prison; please come this way Madam, boy everything's really torn up here Madam, all of this needs a lot of help, really a lot; our fields are gone and at this point our houses have gotten turned into mud and trash on the valley floor over there; and the money we got from the Project to make good on our losses, wellllll that's why it's called making good on our losses because we good and lost what can you do Madam; but we can't say this because it would put our families in danger, we could get stamped Communist Party member or OK-EM[10] on our identity cards, whoa that's a real disaster Madam if you get stamped like that, that's it! You're like someone thrown into prison on Kambangan Island and you haven't a hope for anything anymore; but we still have God don't we, we're convinced He won't abandon us even though I don't know nowadays it seems like the winners are always the sleazy ones, maybe these are the End Times but don't say that out loud Madam; better we just work hard, and we'll have to see how things go, because there's a bunch of gutsy people, they want to go to court Madam, but their chances are like a snowball's in hell Madam, I mean a great big zero; hey the fact of the matter is that the little people always lose even if they're in the right, but once again there is still God, even though funny how God doesn't do anything; and we haven't a clue where we're going to go; sorry Madam but better stay here in the middle of the path if you get too far over to the side you might fall off the cliff, just take it easy Madam, even though it's not rainy and it's not slippery the soil often gives way because it's loose and chalky Madam; sorry but we'll just make our way around that little hill to the back of it; don't be startled Madam, because we're just refugees so we just have to make do, we'll settle for a hut to keep a roof over our heads, although it's too bad about our kids actually, it's been almost a year they haven't been able to go to school because the school buildings that were put up a couple of years before the project started up got leveled to the ground Madam, the project did that two years ago, well that's what they're like, so we're forced into transmigrating; but why should we transmigrate to the middle of the jungle while they get to put up hotels on our land and all kinds of businesses swimming in money, are we

---

10.  OK=Organisasi Kiri [Leftist Organization]; EM=Eks Merah [Ex-Red].

getting sacrificed or what, now that isn't in line with Pancasila, isn't that right, Madam; but sorry maybe I'm talking too much, forgive me who are you Madam, it isn't that I'm curious, it's just a matter of courtesy you know: if I don't know your name and who you are it's as though I'm not taking proper care and serving you . . . oh I see, so Madam is an inspector checking up on the Project okay, ooh I'm so sorry Madam, what I just said was just shooting the breeze nothing serious, please let's just pretend I never said it Madam. Oh okay okay thank you thank you for your kindness Madam, thank you for not reporting what I said; well you know we're just dumb farmers so we don't often know what it is we're supposed to say, Madam. Nussy looked ahead sadly, as though she was no longer aware of walking, as if she was no longer in that place, she felt so weak and exhausted. Oh, there was no way her brother Brojol could recognize his younger sister Iin after so many dozens of years and after so many incidents, the plastic surgery especially separated them from their past; from that time in Magelang's world where the KNIL still had their barracks and their mother squatted in front of the Chinese temple selling fried cassava snacks and sometimes she invited little Iin to go to the Muslim quarter near the mosque near the canal to buy her some stewed jackfruit and rice with chicken only a thin little strip of it or just a quarter of an egg; oh a time when they were poor but funny it seems like she was happier than now that she's become a billionaire in dollars but by dint of giant projects like this one that are murdering her own twin brother. So what is she going to say if indeed her brother can't recognize her anymore?

# Chapter Seven

It was clear, just as she had feared, of course Brother Brojol didn't recognize his younger sister whose face and form were so different as a result of the Singapore operation and after so many dozens of years without meeting or sending each other photos. Even though she thought beforehand that she was pretty well prepared for it, still at the moment she met up with her brother again Iin couldn't keep from crying, so everybody was amazed what was the matter; oh maybe she's sick because of the hot sun or from walking, because of course a great lady isn't used to hiking around in the hills and in the blazing sun; thus the local women took the important guest into the room for newlyweds next to the storage room for rice, Goddess Sri's chamber, although of course given the circumstances everything was modest in the extreme; so that she could rest a bit and recover from the heat of the sun. Brother Brojol himself was surprised how was it the foreign lady was looking for him, and truly surprised asked himself and of course got asked by his wife who sensibly enough suddenly *sa-kal*[1] got bitten by the jealousy virus, who was that gorgeous woman who looked like Goddess Umayi? And if she really did have the status of an inspector what was she

---

1. Suddenly at that time [Javanese].

doing coming to the place where the local inhabitants had sought
shelter, and not going to the Project office over there in the valley
where ducking and ramming going back and forth so many thousands of dump trucks and so many hundreds of tractors were scrap-
ing and clawing and turning under the rice fields that belonged to
*the villagers* that the Project manager types had taken over without
consultation without regard for custom and proper procedures; and
stranger still then the lady just cried and moaned, cried and sighed
and moaned in the room so that Brother Brojol's mother-in-law who
was very old but still had all her wits about her could only shake her
head, what's the matter, shaking her head; there that's enough now
she should drink some water flavored with the nutmeg someone was
told to run go get from the old curer; and sure enough the nutmeg
and honey drink did finally put the lady guest to sleep, without getting out of her clothes without bathing without eating without asking for anything. Ms. Driver left waiting got called by a delegation
of men women and youths; in this way, once assurances had been
given by a group of youths responsible for local security that the jeep
would be safe from children's naughty hands or for that matter bad
guys' malevolent ones, the diminutive but feisty Srikandi of a Ms.
Driver followed them to the displaced people's makeshift hamlet.
But the diminutive but mannish Ms. Driver remained silent in a thousand languages, and in the face of all kinds of questioning tactics
employed by the local women the good woman did not say who
she was in accordance with the very strict instructions she had
received from *Madame* de Proguelêaux before they had set out.

All afternoon and evening dozens of children spied on her
through the door windows gaps in the bedroom's boards to see just
what the white radish lady with a long straight carrot nose was doing
in the bedroom on the sleeping platform; and of course they got
chased away broomed away slapped away by their mothers and older
sisters, but naturally it isn't that easy to chase away flies, and eventually the ones telling them to stop got annoyed and fed up and tired

of it and then left them alone to go on spying staring and acting stupefied, they were just hillbilly kids never having seen a lady like a clown, they'll tire of it eventually; but which kids were getting tired of it, they kept taking turns spying and stealing looks waving their fingers to call their friends then whispering in their ears and looking some more and looking at each other; some of them got teary-eyed rubbed their eyes then ran off; true enough eventually they got tired of it or were embarrassed to be seen shedding tears, because the woman just lay there crying; they had never seen an adult cry for such a long time and with such emotion and here it hadn't been preceded by a fight or a lot of name-calling like with their mothers or older sisters; but city people are always strange so just leave her be, anything city people do must be proper and correct and it shouldn't be surprising, after all they're just hillbilly kids so really what's surprising really it's the kids themselves, that's what their mothers and older sisters said; whereas Brother Brojol's mother-in-law just shook her head but full of respectful concern and full of protective feelings for the woman guest who had to be a very important person. But once the tractors and the dump trucks stopped working, before the sun set, the guest took her leave and couldn't be persuaded cajoled constrained into staying the night since it would soon be dark, and so forth and so on and so forth and so on. Thus after an hour of being cajoled and urged and appealed to not to go home yet and please have a rest because here we've gotten hot water ready for your bath and so forth and so on nevertheless nothing worked, the two guests left, accompanied by all the kids and a big portion of the adults and young people from the displaced people's hamlet. But unseen by anyone Madam had secretly pressed and pressured Mrs. Brother Brojol's Mother-in-Law into accepting a little package she gave her that she was not allowed to open till after the jeep had left.

Thus once the diminutive but feisty Srikandi driver had started the jeep then put it in gear then revved up the gas then pointed it in the direction of the city beyond the hills and heaps, and after the

evening prayers, only then did the kindly old Mrs. Mother-in-Law
work up the nerve to open the package, immediately screamed and
fainted, yes fainted. Brother Brojol was stunned and everyone in the
house ran to her room and found Dear Mother-in-Law in a faint next
to Niyah who was yelling with the open package containing oh oh
my oh my oh good God, after a rough count and Mrs. Mother-in-
Law conscious again, there turned out to be exactly seventeen million rupiahs, *duh Gusti duh Gusti nyuwun wilujeng.*[2] Once the dear Mrs.
Mother-in-Law explained that this wasn't stolen money and that it
really was a gift from the strange lady, Granny Mother-in-Law
asserted that she didn't want to keep this money for herself but better that it be used for the needs of the people now suffering misfortune in the displaced people's hamlet. Brother Brojol agreed and even
his wife nodded her agreement, because it was safer that way and
no doubt it really was intended for the whole hamlet and not just
for Granny Pa Brojol's Mother-in-Law alone. Everybody who had
come swarming around from the other huts because they heard Brojol's wife screaming and yelling voiced their agreement with the decision; and this proved once again that the All-Just and Loving God
exists and that Madam was certainly the Angel Gabriel or somebody,
anyway this was surely at the command of the All-Beneficent and
All-Just God; for the time being the children watched all these goings
on with gaping mouths and wide-open eyes, they didn't understand
what the adults were talking about; what mattered was that today
was a special day and they had seen a jeep completely unlike the
ones owned by the Project that went by a lot, and it turns out the
driver really was a woman, and this was more amazing than everything else, especially for the girls who only knew how to look for
firewood and herd the goats and wash dirty pants and fry cassava.
But the men stayed up late into the night discussing Joyoboyo and

2.  My dear Lord, I beg your mercy [Javanese].

Ronggowarsito and Queen Kencana Wungu and Ken Dedes and the
Angel Gabriel, and they were surprised a woman dressed like a clown
would own that much money, surely she wasn't really a Project
Inspector, because they were their enemies and what enemy would
give them a present of seventeen million rupiahs; so the only one
who knew the real angle the twists and turns of this was Brother
Brojol, since from the very start the guest had talked about and asked
where Pa Brojol's house was.

But Pa Brojol himself was at a loss, what could he answer his
friends and buddies, because cross his heart and hope to die he didn't
know that mysterious woman; fortunately Mrs. Mother-in-Law
had calmed his wife down persuading her this was no case of having
a woman on the side or anything, because a kept woman behaves
completely differently, thus Mrs. Mother-in-Law had explained
everything to her own daughter and to others, so let's just hope everything's settled; but Brother Brojol and the whole hamlet, and later
the whole village and subdistrict, still asked in amazement: who on
earth could it have been; boy it's really true these days there's all kinds
of stories and plots, everything's at cross-purposes and confused
there's no guidelines anymore, there's no sense, there's no tradition;
well so maybe that's it and you have to rest assured, everything will
turn out to have its reasons because God's ways are beyond humans'
grasp; thus one by one they took their leave to go sleep in their own
shacks, only some of them stayed and sprawled out anywhere, falling
fast asleep on the sleeping platforms till the sun was pretty high in
the sky; waking up surprised to find things were the same as usual,
with their farmer colleagues who always smelled of farmyard dung,
and their wives who didn't wear long pants, no dark glasses even
though their skin and faces were already dark as the heart of a hardwood tree or dark as the rice fields' soil, so by rights it would be fitting
and proper if they wore dark glasses, but the fact was the only dark
thing about them was their hair and their eyes which weren't as
attractive as that woman's who fell from the sky yesterday, who dis-

appeared unfortunately so there was nothing left to watch except there was still stuff to talk about, and especially puzzling questions still unanswered, including for Pa Brojol himself who in light of the incident yesterday was getting steadily more popular but was also getting steadily more closely watched by his wife, well so who *was* that yesterday?

It was really strange, why would a Project Inspector cry like that, what did she have to cry about; the ones with the right to cry were the ones driven off by the Project right, really, it was a puzzle for the village dwellers who had been driven off their land but still defended their rights as citizens and didn't want to transmigrate because they did not accept having foreigners come with hundreds of tractors and thousands of dump trucks without engaging them in consultation without engaging in respectful discussion as is right, just to scrape up all the millions of rupiahs of profits as they pleased, while telling the ones who got driven off they had to go clear the dense jungle wild and far from everything, well easy for them to say; because aside from all of the above, there's also the point that a lot of the older citizens wouldn't have the strength to work hard in the jungle which is very tough to cultivate, and for that reason a lot of the oldsters like Pa Brojol's mother-in-law had entrusted themselves to the Lord God, "Go ahead and transmigrate if you wish, I haven't got the strength; go ahead and go if you have the heart to leave your widowed mother to live all alone in a shack on the slopes of a chalk mountain that's dry dusty desertous go ahead, but your mother wants to keep watch at the place of your grandparents and ancestors who were buried over there although they've gotten dug up disturbed crushed crunched by those tractors and dump trucks; fine let them be cursed with misfortune, but if you people want to go, go ahead go ahead your mother won't stop you.

Meanwhile far away from Brojol's hamlet absolutely resolute decided determined our worthy "Inspector," that is Iin Sulinda Pertiwi Punyo Nusamusbida alias Charlotte Eugenie *Madame* de Pro-

guelêaux née du Bois de la Montagne intended to respond personally herself with a clear approach above reproach to the great conun-
drum thrown up by the vagaries of history. Thus on the second day after those children had encountered
the all-new sparkling shiny jeep which when peered into turned out
to be carrying many thermoses, some of them containing brown and
yellow ice cream and cakes of all varieties all wrapped up, Punyo
the self-proclaimed Project Inspector was sitting in an air-conditioned
meeting room in Singapore, consulting with the extremely famous
head of the plastic surgery clinic who had metamorphosed Tiwi into
Nusamusbida a while back (back when Dr. Soebandrio and Air Force
General Omar Dhani were being Special 30th of September court-
martialed), about Madam's strange request that her pretty face and
all the rest: head, hair, breasts, waist, hips, legs, all of it get changed
back to the way it was originally like before the plastic surgery, so
that in short her form and features all of them would once again
become Iin Sulinda Pertiwi. The noted specialist professor, clearing
his throat and nodding as a sign of his complete understanding of a
woman's wants which like the wind in Singapore also change direction a lot, had someone bring him a thick comprehensive folder of
documentation that had been archived in this way even though it
had also been microfilmed as well, in which was retained a complete record of all parts and details of the whole body and especially
the face of the VIP lady client before him; and once all the photos
and data had been projected on a large screen on the wall as well as
on a computer screen and studied thoroughly while continuing to
clear his throat and nod his head, at last the eminent Team Chief
specialist professor nodded extra deeply once without clearing his
throat and said briefly but weightily: *"Yes! It's possible, Madame."*
    Thus once she had paid who knows how many hundreds of thou-
sands or millions of Singapore dollars, *Madame* de Proguelêaux disappeared into the sophisticated clinic complex in a meditation
program like a cocoon, to emerge a month later, exactly when they

were having a big National Resurgence Day ceremony in Jakarta celebrated by thousands of young schoolchildren in Senayan Stadium, so out she came like usually happens with a cocoon, as if she were a patented copy of a native butterfly, exactly identical in all details from organs to face most of all: Iin Linda Pertiwi, complete with her old name so full of meaning as is customary for people of Javanese descent: Nusamusbida, Punyo Nusamusbida; and carrying a super important folder containing 19 documents with official stamps, and 45 pages, signed by a team consisting of 8 plastic surgeons accompanied by their assistants, 17 authentic witnesses including a notary exercising full authority, who asserted unequivocally in an official capacity it was recognized by International Law, that the person of Iin Sulinda Pertiwi Nusamusbida was fully and entirely identical with the person of Charlotte Eugenie de Proguelêaux née du Bois de la Montagne, and by the same token Charlotte and etcetera and etcetera and etcetera, also identical with Angelin Ruth Portier and Tukinah Senik and etcetera and etcetera and etcetera.

Thus once she had spent a month's vacation in a charming tourist city, Chiang Mai in Thailand, feeling completely satisfied and confident that she was not making a single mistake, Miss Bi flew to Bangkok, to the luxurious five-star Oriental Hotel on the banks of the Chao Phya River, rented an apartment on the very top floor, all of this as per the *top-secret* information instructions of her secretary who's old and decrepit but knows all the addresses of the Mafia, Triad, Yakuza, syndicates and spy networks of all nations, in order to have a *rendezvous* with (ah now this was Miss Bi's one biggest and fatalest mistake ignoring that decrepit old secretary's advice), well a secret meeting with . . . the former bald youth with the wooden rifle back in the Seinendan-Keibodan days, who likewise was still active as a double agent both patriotic and commercial, in order to ask for a new passport; even though the secretary said, that if it was just to make a fake passport she had a friend a former Vietcong who was an expert. But for some reason, maybe at that time

Miss Bi, after so many months without getting intimate with any sons of Adam, was thirsty for that biological cocaine heroin; and what's more understandable, wished to celebrate her metamorphosis turning into an authentic Nusantara butterfly with *her first love* from the days of youthful romance and revolutionary romance, because everything that had gone into the decision to change herself from *Madame* de Proguelêaux and etcetera and etcetera into Ibu Nusamusbida could be considered and intended as a form of revolution too, albeit individual.

And it happened he showed up our *double agent* whose name must still be kept secret, suffice it to use his code SBSD-45 (Secret Bureau of Strategic Decodifications) in the apartment of our Great Butterfly cheerful outgoing very charming, altogether different from back when he was still carrying a wooden rifle, or when they were in Hong Kong: he had gotten a bit older but was safeguarded by the technology of hair dye, *face foundations,* and *makeup* from the famous Rubinstein cosmetics company, which made SBSD-45 look like he was still at the age of 40 plus five, and by the same token: thanks to the expertise of the plastic surgery clinic in Singapore Miss Bi herself came across as if she were aged 40 minus five, at the height of her late-youth's beauty which was more convincing than when she had important positions in (not too loud, just whisper it) Lekra and Gerwani. And they teased each other a bit, the two veterans, but relatively discreetly these young people did, joking, kidding each other, and shooting the breeze about the old days, drinking in an unfeigned nostalgia for the days when they were still poor; well like all *new riches* do anywhere in reunions sometimes mentioning old friends who are still just getting by because they're dim and don't know how to manipulate situations, well maybe that's just the share allotted them by the Law of Karma and so forth and so on. Obviously at just the right moment, and for people like them obviously the rightest moment was on their love bed, the matter of a new passport came up whispered softly obscenely into SBSD-45's ear, in accordance with his double nature he gave her the okay signal with regard to the event of Angelin Ruth Charlotte Eugenie's returning to the lap of Mother Pertiwi with a kiss in the name of National Resurgence Day; in the events of that moment of course "Mr. Pertiwa" was happy as a clam but not without a certain commercial element, because well these are the days of professional everything; thus this time it got measured in yen, because the dollar kept getting weaker. Okay okay, about the cost, *no problem!*

For three more days and nights in line with traditional Javanese celebrations they celebrated the event of their shacking up together in a snakes' nest on the banks of the very interesting Chao Phya River. Yes, Bangkok is the most appropriate city for anyone who wants to pay homage to the Goddess of Filth, so everything should be done with style and class, not just lunging for one another. She was happy Iin Miss Bi was for some unknown reason, maybe because her twin's blood finally did really make her very much miss her brother Brojol who would certainly recognize her again now; oh Brother Brojol whom she had once been jealous of because he could fool around and wander about as he pleased, whereas poor little Iin had to cook, wash the dishes, sweep the floor, just because Iin was a girl; but that's all over let bygones be bygones don't keep digging it up, in fact in the end due to Iin being forced to work in the kitchen and at the well back then, Auntie Wi Miss Bi developed determination and guts, such that she could see all corners of the world, had mounted all the world's wonders and could have interchange and intercourse with so many important figures, well-known figures, international figures, movie star figures, in a word mattress experience but mattresses in the class of the Ritz Hotel in Paris or the Waldorf-Astoria; it's really true the Law of Karma allots very different shares, there's no reason for people to feel envious actually, especially social envy; there are those whose duty it is to be filthy rich and there are those whose noble mission it is to be poor, but the two are two poles of a single sphere, two-in-one the great universe in its entirety, Yin and Yang, Pendawa

Kurawa; now at a certain moment Yin has to meet with Yang, and how great was her homesickness, it was almost unbearable, Iin wanted so much to reenter her beloved Homeland, to meet with Brother Brojol, much as, although in a different context, Queen Banowati of the Kurawa court longed melancholic for Arjuna.

# Chapter Eight

But jumping for joy and getting so overly self-confident that you forget to be wary is never a good thing, and this is what happened to Punyo Nusamusbida. In the *VIP-class* cabin Mrs. Nus got help putting her carry-on bag in the compartment above her seat from a friendly Indonesian *gentleman* who was neatly dressed in the very latest fashion, wearing a golden tie, she guessed it was a creation of the designer Rei Kawakubo who enchanted Mrs. Nus with his very artful diamond pins that sparkled and gleamed so beautifully, promising a very memorable first meeting, especially because the *gentleman* spoke Indonesian with an accent *à la* Parangakik so she learned from a brief and courteous but cordial exchange, that he was a young Ph.D. in macroeconomics who had just finished his degree *cum laude*[1] from the University of the Sorbonne, while revealing in all humility that he had been sent by the Central Planning Board's Chief Minister on a mission regarding maintaining economic ties to the European Economic Union in Brussels and to lobby several important members of the European Parliament in Strasbourg; here truly was a prospective new contact that could be interesting, thought Punyo Managing Director Lindy Nusamusbida as she read his name card

---

1. With commendation.

stamped with the National Garuda symbol and attractive gold hand-lettering closely. The whole way from Bangkok to Jakarta the good *Gentleman* with a politesse that was enchanting and reminded Mrs. Nus of some of the gestures and style of the one who always showed up in her dreams when she was feeling lonely, that is *le noble Cheva-lier de la désirée*[2] who climbs the ladder and comes in through her window bearing a handful of red roses and white jasmine and who strangely enough always turns up in the same way but his face keeps changing; anyway the attitude and demeanor of this noble young *Gentleman* with the Rei Kawakubo tie and gleaming diamond pins really looked a lot like that guy in her dreams, thus she felt pleased at the glitteringly positive signs flying this time on an Airbus 300, thanks to the presence of the young doctor in macroeconomics who really got her attention like a thousand megawatt magnet when he talked about kidding around with Margareth Thatcher or Steffi Graf, of stories from when he was a personal guest of the Kennedy family and the Nehru dynasty; and too about a theory concerning the tendency for the center of gravity of economic activity to shift from Europe to Asia and the Pacific; so with high hopes Mrs. Nus invited the good *Gentleman* who was polite and refined like an aris-tocrat, to please come visit sometime at her bungalow in Puncak and so forth and so on; to which he responded respectfully but it seemed clear his heart was moved to respond to her invitation with elegant graciousness in a language redolent of palace diplomacy yet filling the heart with yearning, and Nusimus was convinced that she wasn't old yet, really not yet.

Thus they arrived at the superhuge and awe-inspiring Soekarno-Hatta Airport which could be likened without a stretch to the Senayan Stadium in the old days: Bung Karno's Passion (and Bung Hatta's Travail). The *gentleman* helped her again taking down her

---

2. Noble knight the object of one's desire.

carry-on bag from the compartment above her seat, and politely invited Punyo Lindy Nusamusbida to go ahead of him out the VIP exit, going down the steps; politely once again *our gentleman* suggested that she not walk under the plane's wing, because that often had undesirable effects on one's health and even they say puts one at risk for cancer. Mrs. Nus followed the advice of the noble young *chevalier* who was so nice and *galant* taking notice of all these little things, something that always works like a charm for Adam's sons with every former Adam's rib, well thereupon it happened an unexpected event under the tip of that big wing, when Punyo Lindy Nusamusbida was greeted with especial respect by two uniformed officers who apparently knew the good *Gentleman* well; well Miss Bi was so startled-stunned she couldn't pronounce a single word, as firmly but still respectfully courteously she was pushed along to the backseat of a VW minivan and handcuffed, while the good *Gentleman* accompanying her sat calmly diplomatically beside the driver and pretended not to see what was being done in an artfully professional manner in the backseat; presumably so that Punyo *Madame* wouldn't feel ashamed he was silent in a thousand and one languages, really this was too crushing, so Miss Bi wept, the Law of Karma oh the Law of Karma she moaned in her heart, indeed the history of the great teaches us how the greatest success often constitutes the turning point toward a tragic fall; for example Bung Karno and others; *wel, als het moet,*[3] if this is indeed the fate scratched out for Iin Sulinda Pertiwi Nusamusbida, then this too she would confront as in the manner of a Margareth Thatcher or more likely Benazir Bhutto confronting any hardship; it would not be for nothing that Iin Sulinda was the daughter of the sole *heiho* who overcame the sea that time, even though his ship full of sacks of Dutch coins sank and the whole Japanese platoon croaked.

---

3. Well, if this is how it must be.

After she had been interrogated by an intelligence major who had the face of a wild boar but the mouth of a myna bird who showed her several old photos from the previous Order, in which Iin Sulinda Pertiwi could be seen leading Lekra members in a demonstration to smash Malaysia and giving a speech on Madiun's town square urging people to hang the comprador bureaucrat capitalists, as well as photos of her at the Beijing airport together with Red Hammer figures in front of a plane carrying tens of thousands of rifles for the 5$^{th}$ Force; and obviously all the pictures in those old photos looked like Miss Bi, even though there was a little difference between the way she put her hair in a bun then and her hair's *coiffure* now, thus it was clear how useless it would be to deny it; that indeed this Mrs. Nusamusbida was once a Lekra and Gerwani leader, she admitted to all of that, without crying without moaning except for one tear that she quietly wiped away sadly, because she realized that given a new situation like this Sis Iin would not be able to meet her twin brother Pa Brojol again whom she missed, the sole historical witness to when Miss Bi was still little Iin; furthermore she wouldn't be able to mention Brojol's name in front of these officials, because for sure if she did Brojol would die straightaway struck by a clean-environment lightning operation, because twins are obviously more closely related than grandchildren or children of parents-in-law who are already reason enough for people to be "cleaned" from the surface of the Indonesian earth which is dearly loved but disgraces itself too easily in its suspicions. Thus Iin waited and waited in her jail cell, which was supplied only with a set of readings the Koran, the Protestant-Catholic Bible and the Bhagawad Gita, while all of her things and papers which she had brought with her were seized doubtless examined by the security officials; maybe there would be names full of implications jotted down in her date book, maybe in a copied letter; this much was clear: three days later the capital city's papers and the News Program on TV broadcast the happy news both surprising and heartening that a dangerous fugitive from justice a former woman leader of Lekra and Gerwani had been caught in a brilliant fashion by means of the care and diligence of the nation's intelligence services with the help of the citizenry; this news was also taken up by foreign mass media and Amnesty International so a furious polemic exploded overseas in the papers and bulletins which are indeed "free and liberal," printed and published without a Letter of Authorization to Print or Permit to Operate a Press. Since she had nothing to do in her cell, just to pass the time Miss Bi read flipping about in all the Holy Books provided in the cell, 17 pages each day in each book, finishing up with devout prayers for Brother Brojol and his wife and children and the inhabitants of the refugee camp, while feeling happy thankful and singing God's praises inasmuch as in this way the giant tourist and study center Disneyland project in their village would be stopped and the land returned to its rightful inhabitants, because 90% of the shares were in her hands.

However the story's not over yet, the *kayon* signaling the end of the shadow play hasn't gotten stuck in the middle of the banana tree trunk yet, because the story continues: one morning one April and one year before the year 2000 five officials came by, one of them the pretend *gentleman* on the plane who claimed to have a doctorate in economics; they asked over and over was it true that Iin Sulinda Pertiwi Nusamusbida was the same person as Charlotte Eugenie *Madame* de Proguelêaux née du Bois de la Montagne, and vice versa, as they read in a folder containing 19 documents and 45 pages found in the distinguished accused's valise? Quite true, replied Iin resolutely so that the three officials looked at each other in silence; it was evident that they were rather confused confounded conflabbergasted by the discovery of this data which strangely enough had never been examined and checked by SBSD-45 reports; so out they went exiting the cell once the good *Gentleman* had left on the table a gift in the form of an official Interpretive Guide to the Pancasila. Three days later the good *Gentleman* came again with eight other people who stated that according to a decision of those in charge and in authority Madam Nusamusbida was free, but with one condition: namely that she continue the giant Disneyland *à la* Indonesia project that so many parties had already signed off on and which was already well under way; it would be unfortunate if the momentum of such a fine project's construction got bogged down let alone stopped, thus for that purpose the parties in charge and in authority would look for the most effective *modus quo*[4] and legal *status* for the sake of all this, particularly for Mrs. Lindy Nusamusbida, so there you have it; and not forgetting to ask whether Mrs. Nusamusbida could contact two contractor financiers overseas who were very vital for gathering funds for the Project and doing some macroeconomic lobbying with several creditor nations' governments, specifically those named in the Consortium Project agreements, that is *Mevrouw*[5] Angelin Ruth Portier domiciled in Drente, the Netherlands, and a billionaire woman who is never at home in Cokrodiningratan Yogyakarta but she might be a lady from Suriname, that is Mrs. Tukinah Senik; thus would Mrs. Nusamusbida be so kind as to contact those two billionaires in order to reassure them and neutralize the effects of the Soekarno-Hatta incident that had caused a misunderstanding and even landed Mrs. Nusamusbida in jail and the news hurriedly and rashly spread about by socially irresponsible journalists who are only interested in sensationalism; so that the important ladies would be persuaded that there's actually no problem and the Project will continue because the momentum is actually very strong. Miss Bi's heart rejoiced in her triumph, hah this was further proof of how even the daughter of a *heiho* and a fried-cassava-snack seller could reach the stars in the sky without fear of getting hit by men's reckless rockets. "Fine," responded Mrs. Nusamusbida calmly and with great dignity. "But I need time to think it over, because this humiliating incident

---

4. Means how to.
5. Mrs.

cannot simply be forgiven and put aside with polite phrases and easy beg-your-pardons in the gypster-jivey-conjuring-disingenuous Javanese way and that sort of childishness; that even intelligence types need to be careful to not just look out for their own good and to think more comprehensively, don't go handcuffing *VIP-class* passengers in a high-handed fashion; and that it is not the behavior of a *gentleman* to pretend hypocritically to be helping out when he's actually casting an innocent person into misery."

Thus preceded by armored cars and tanks and *voorrijders*[6] of two teams of Military Police sergeant-majors riding the very latest model Harley-Davidsons Mrs. Iin Sulinda Pertiwi Nusamusbida was escorted in a Mercedes limousine with bulletproof windows to the private bungalow she owned in Puncak with its beautiful view; Parihayangan's fertile prosperous valleys, yes it was in this way in this place Iin Sulinda Pertiwi thought about and mused upon what would be best for her to do, because the matter was by no means simple even though Iin was very used to dealing with supertough problems; just imagine, if she chose to continue to involve herself in the project, she would certainly have to go to Singapore again to the plastic surgery clinic because she had had those discussions with the World Bank and other agencies in the guise of Charlotte Eugenie *Madame* de Proguelêaux; it was irritating, every time you change your identity why should you have to change your face, change your hair, change your neck, change your breasts, change your belly, change your behind, change your thighs, change your calves, it was nauseating; but if she didn't, so she kept Iin Sulinda Pertiwi's original indigenous shape like she had now uh-oh the bad news is that would be sure to endanger Brother Brojol who apparently no agency yet knew was her twin brother, for sure he would get turned into a second-degree sacrificial victim, as a result of being related to an ex-leader

---

6. Motorcycle-riding honor guard.

of Lekra and Gerwani; thus to be that cold that cruel Iin didn't have the heart, oh even if Brojol *had* only played around and wandered about shooting at birds with his slingshot and stealing mangoes out of Haji Hammam's yard, even though he always came home with dirty clothes and the buttons gone and the seat of his pants torn and it was Iin always Iin who had to sew them had to put on new buttons had to launder his dirty clothes and wash the dishes her brother had used, still no, not . . . Iin wasn't a revenge-taker like most people of the archipelago; she wasn't a revenge-taker, she was Pertiwi, so said her teacher the future composer who had once taken a shine to her at the Sempoerna Elementary School the former *Bijzondere H.I. School* on Pendowo Street opposite the old Regency Office in Magelang, Goddess Pertiwi that is; (according to a one-day seminar) the active energy sakti of Lord Wisnu, the protector and conserver of life, the guide and counselor the source of well-being and peace and relatedness and so forth; no, Iin wasn't going to endanger Pa Brojol who had already suffered quite enough, in fact she intended to buy back all the land village dry fields irrigated fields houseyards and everything that had been taken over by the Project, in other words she was going to have all 1945 hectares that had already gotten torn up steamrollered ruined turned back into irrigated fields, landscapes and all exactly like they were before, and in addition there would be compensation for all parties that had suffered losses: oh money was really no object, praise be to God she had just been offered a chance to carry out a supply operation, providing several dozen container ships full of parts necessary for erections in Iraq and Libya of atomic reactors and chemical weapons factories and just three transports' trips would be enough to buy back that whole area; but would the authorities permit it? Would this not be a slap in the face for the authorities, causing them to suffer a loss of face, and isn't it the case that suffering a loss of face is the worst form of suffering for Eastern peoples?

A dilemma, Pertiwi led a life in constant dilemmahood, but in

the old days Iin was young, now she was more than half a century
old; was it always going to be like this, playing Durga in Corpstenchfield in Lebanon in Iraq in Cambodia but in her own country too,
spreading a feast of death in order to please her live-in crony Lord
Kala dealing in guns, cocaine and women of ill repute, that is women
of her own kind? Ah the mysteries of virtue! The mysteries of evil!
If Goddess Durga and Lady Umayi were one and the same, was Iin
fated to live a life full of doubles full of dilemmas full of conflicts full
of contradictions without a break for the rest of her life, and why and
what for and to what end? Hadn't there been a breakthrough, hadn't
there resounded a Proclamation of Independence freedom redemp-
tion rescue from some quarter or other? To do away with this distressing dualism? Iin Sulinda Pertiwi Nusamusbida Charlotte Eugenie
de Proguelêaux née du Bois de la Montagne Angelin Ruth Portier Tukinah Senik pondered as she prayed prayers that were crumbly crispy
crumpled hurried hastied hindered, crying and crying crazed confused
chaotic; while before her lay open shut open shut open the Bible the
Koran the Bhagawad Gita and the like, she pondered thinking considering confusedly conflictedly brainstorming and planning what
would be best, pondering possibilities further how best to approach
this matter full of Durga Umayi dilemmas and contradictions . . . and
oh Lord good God, at just that moment of dejected despondency confusion confoundedness when she felt as though tumbled overturned
into an irrevocable ravine, ah just then arrived arose unexpectedly
unsuspectedly, after so many dozens of years of being away, obviously out of rage-become-reserve hearing news reviews about the
behavior of Ms. Durga getting the better of Umayi, oh it turns out he
still remembers her the guy the old old friend, ah *mon noble Chevalier,
que je rêve désiréuse de vous, oui de vous,* the Microphone of 56 East
Pegangsaan Street, forgive forgive your errant traveler, stroke my
cheeks wet with tears with your handsome elegant resonating chamber a patient accepting go-between, speak command instruct . . .
hooong ngo'ahoo, wilahoong hunglawi, oh oh I'in Sulinda Sundali

Pertiwi Perwita, girl gril, capable pacable pretty prinded, child chiled, inexperienced inprexerienced, proclamation macroplation pronouncement mentoprounce, seventeenth nevenseenth August Gaustus, nineteen neentine, fortyfive fiteyvor, may aym, your heart tyouhear, be at peace peaceatbe, oooh ho'oo Pertiwi Perwita, sweet weest, lovely volley, traveler tervelar, seeker keeser, of signs fo nigns, at the four hotherauf, compass points passcom spoint, genuine ingenue, freedom fromeed, oooh oho'o I'in Ni'I, amennn manen menamenn namenenn nanemennn enamennnnnnnn. . . .

There you have it.

# About the Author

Yusuf B. Mangunwijaya was born on May 6, 1929, in the town of Ambarawa, Central Java. Afer graduating from the Sancti Pauli Institute of Philosophy and Theology in Yogyakarta in 1959, he continued his studies at the Rhein-Westfalen Technical School, Aachen, Germany, finishing in 1966. In 1978, this quite productive priest-cum-intellectual was a Fellow at the Aspen Institute for Humanistic Studies, in Aspen, Colorado, USA. Since 1967 he has been a Visiting Professor at the University of Gajah Mada.

In addition to his frequent contributions to the mass media, Mangunwijaya has written several fiction and nonfiction books. His nonfiction books include *Ragawidya* (1975), *Roro Mendut's Cigarette Butts* (1978), *An Introduction to Construction Physics* (1980), *Literature and Religiosity* (1982), *Panca Pramana* (1982), *Fostering Children's Religious Attitudes* (1986), *Wastucitra* (1986) and *In the Shadow of the Lord* (1987). He edited two volumes of *Technology and Its Cultural Impact* (1983 and 1985).

His publications in fiction are *Father Rahadi* (1981), *The Weaverbirds* (1981), *Sharks, Minnows and Tuna* (1983), the *Roro Mendut Trilogy* (1983), *Genduk Duku* (1987), *Lusi Lindri* (1987), and the *Ballad of the Pedicab* (1985).

---

[This brief, unsigned biography of Mangunwijaya appears at the end of the original Indonesian edition of the novel.]

Mangunwijaya has received many awards for his writings, both within and outside Indonesia. One of his short stories was chosen in the Golden Windmill Competition, sponsored by Netherlands Radio, and published together with other winning short stories in a collection entitled *Dari Jodoh Sampai Supiyah* (1976). In 1982 *Literature and Religiosity* won first prize in the essay category from the Jakarta Arts Council. And his novel *The Weaverbirds* won the 1983 SEA Write Award from Queen Sirkit of Thailand.

His stature abroad is also reflected in the fact that *Sharks, Minnows and Tuna* was translated into Dutch, and *The Weaverbirds* into English, Japanese, and Dutch.

In his role as priest-engineer, Mangunwijaya has not only published a number of books concerning technology and architecture but was also entrusted with the task of designing a number of important buildings, such as the headquarters of the Defence Territorial Command, the Bishopric of Semarang, and a number of churches and private homes. As a spiritual leader, his convictions have often impelled him to speak out forcefully and to become a committed social activist. In early 1986 he tenaciously defended the impoverished residents living along the Code River in Yogyakarta, when they were about to be driven from their homes in the name of urban renewal. And recently he has been very much involved in the humanitarian efforts on behalf of people in the region of Kedung Ombo.

# Translator's Notes

## Foreshadowplay

The images that fill the right-hand margins of the pages on which the prose poem is printed are taken from several beautifully illustrated volumes about Javanese shadow plays published in Batavia (now Jakarta) in the early twentieth century. They have been reprinted many times since in Indonesia. The characters that appear are all readily identifiable to shadow play enthusiasts. Each image is reproduced singly at the start of one chapter of the novel, and each one, as it appears, will be identified individually in these notes. The prose poem itself, which begins the novel, corresponds to the opening portion of a shadow play performance. This consists of a long introduction, lasting at least twenty minutes, in which the puppet master alternately sings snippets of old Javanese poetry and intones in florid words a description of the kingdom in which the story opens. Few spectators will understand more than a small portion of the arcane vocabulary that the puppet master pronounces. But the point is not so much to convey information as to set the scene, with the puppet master's voice blending with the gamelan orchestra's accompaniment in an enveloping wash of sound. In this prose poem, Mangunwijaya plays on the line between intelligibility and barely intelligible sound as he reviews the well-known story of how the Lord Guru and his consort Goddess Umayi cursed each other to take on monstrous forms.

**p. 19** *Arjun's Honeyrealm* refers to the kingdom ruled by Arjuna, third of the five Pandawa brothers in the *Mahabharata*.

**p. 19** *Noble Lord Brilliantjewel Maharaja of Heaven* refers to Batara Guru, the name by which Siva is known throughout the Indonesian archipelago. He is considered the chief of the gods in Javanese tradition.

**p. 20** *Ngarcapada* refers to the world between heaven and the underworld in the shadow play tradition, that is, the world humans inhabit.

**p. 20** *Sakti* is understood in Indonesian and Javanese to mean extraordinary potency and is usually applied to powerful males or to potent objects, such as daggers or royal regalia usually associated with males. Here, however, Mangunwijaya uses it in its Sanskrit meaning, referring to the great if ambiguous power of the feminine.

## Chapter One

The image at the beginning of this chapter is of a shadow play character named Mustikawèni. The way she holds her head high, rather than with the downcast eyes of a more refined female figure, shows that she is self-confident or even headstrong. She tried to avenge her ancestor's death by taking on the form of the son of one of the righteous Pandawa brothers and duplicitously obtaining a mystically potent document in the Pandhawas' possession. Her stratagem was ultimately laid bare, but only after it caused many mishaps and misunderstandings.

**p. 25, n. 2** *Sutan Takdir Alisjahbana* was a novelist and philosopher. He worked as an editor at the Balai Pustaka, a government commission that promoted literacy through publications in Malay, Sundanese, and Javanese, and he cofounded the journal *Peodjangga Baru,* or "New Literatus." He also did much to promote the spread of the Indonesian language, which was a bureaucratically established version of Malay. Malay had served for centuries as a lingua franca among the peoples of the Indonesian archipelago, but this "Market Malay" was thought crude and grammatically irregular by both the Dutch authorities and indigenous members of the colonial bureaucracy, who set about systematizing it.

**p. 25** *Puan:* Indonesians rarely use names without titles preceding them, but there are many titles in circulation and selecting one can prove thorny. *Puan* is a largely archaic title placed before the name of a female aristocrat, whereas *nyonya* was used as a title for a Dutch woman and other high-status but socially distant women. Using the former title, *puan,* would show the speaker's commitment to old forms, thought more authentically indigenous, but the usage would be so unusual as to sound quite peculiar. So the narrator suggests the still more peculiar, because completely invented, conflation of the two terms in *punyo.*

**p. 26** The *Maiden Mendut* and *Pronocitro* were lovers in a tragic story dating from the seventeenth century. Mendut was a beautiful young woman betrothed against her will to an older aristocrat named Wiroguno. She refused to marry him, however, and in response he obliged her to pay him a daily fee. She did this by selling cigarettes she had held in her lips. But when she and her lover, Pronocitro, tried to elope, they were discovered. Wiroguno had Pronocitro stabbed with a *kris* (a Javanese dagger), and Mendut seized the same dagger and killed herself. This story interested Rama Mangunwijaya deeply: he wrote a novel based on it, *Roro Mendut* (Jakarta: Gunung Agung, 1968), and a screenplay for a popular film by the same title. See Barbara Hatley, "Texts and Contexts: The Roro Mendut Folk Legend on Stage and Screen," in K. Sen, ed., *Histories and Stories: Cinema in New Order Indonesia* (Clayton, Australia: Monash University Centre of Southeast Asian Studies/Australia-Indonesia Association).

**p. 26** *Ken Dedes,* according to a well-known Javanese legend, was a very beautiful woman married to the king of Singosari, in eastern Java. A village youth, Ken Arok, went to the capital and entered the king's service. He was made a gardener, but when he caught sight of Ken Dedes he thought himself—younger and handsomer than the king—more deserving of her. Ken Dedes came to feel the same, and together they conspired against the king. Ken Arok learned that in order to obtain the most potent possible dagger, he must go to Empu Gandring, a very powerful *kris* maker. Impressed by Ken Arok's position as a servant at the king's court, Empu Gandring showed him great respect. He informed Ken Arok that it would take a month for the *kris* to be readied for him. Ken Arok went off but became impatient, and when the dagger was made but not yet empowered by its maker, Ken Arok took it and killed Empu Gandring with it. A magic voice then pronounced a curse: Ken Arok himself would be killed by the *kris,* and so would each of his descendants for seven generations after him. Sure enough: he murdered the king, but the king's son, whom Ken Dedes was already carrying in her womb, grew up and killed Ken Arok with the *kris.* Then Ken Arok's son by Ken Dedes killed his half-brother, and so it went for generation after generation.

**pp. 26–27** *Bung Karno* is how Indonesia's first president, Sukarno, was popularly known. (*Su-* is prefixed to many Javanese names; it is understood to mean "superior." But it is also often omitted, so that Sukarno is referred to as "Bung Karno.") The title "Bung" was widely used during the Indonesian Revolution; its use indicates equality among males, unlike the more respectful, and thus hierarchical, Javanese titles "Pak" (for "father") and "Mas" (for "older brother"). But "Bung" has fallen into disuse, in part because hierarchical impulses have triumphed in contemporary Indonesia over the egalitarian ones that the nationalist struggle fostered. Sukarno was considered very handsome, and in accordance with long-standing Javanese assumptions about the politically powerful, he was also believed sexually very potent, able to couple with females both living and legendary. Many Indonesians found his oratory electrifying, and he was fond of identifying himself as "the extension of the tongue of the Indonesian masses."

**p. 27** *VOC:* Dutch traders first reached present-day Indonesia at the end of the sixteenth century. The Dutch East Indies Company, or VOC, was formed in 1602 to regulate Dutch trade with the region. It went bankrupt at the end of the eighteenth century, but the Dutch government then took over its administrative functions and continued to rule the islands until the Japanese forced the Dutch to surrender in 1942. Sukarno read out the Indonesian Proclamation of Independence on August 17, 1945. This date has been celebrated every year since as Independence Day. After the Dutch recognized Indonesia's independence in 1949, Indonesia initiated a period of parliamentary democracy. This was found wanting, however, due to the increasing divisiveness among political parties, and in 1959 Sukarno replaced it with what he termed "Guided Democracy," a far more authoritarian arrangement.

**p. 28** The *Royal Netherlands Indies Army,* or KNIL *(Koninklijk Nederlandsch-Indisch Leger),* was formed in the early nineteenth century and was made up of Dutch, other European, and indigenous "Indies" troops. It participated in efforts to quash the Indonesian revolutionaries in the late 1940s and was disbanded in 1950.

**p. 28** A *pedicab* is a three-wheeled bicycle in which one or more passengers sit on a wide seat while a man seated behind them pedals. Long a major means of transport in towns and cities, and a way for the very poorest males to try to make a living, the pedicab has become less common because of the many motorcycles and cars that now crowd Indonesia's streets.

**p. 28** *Oei Tiong Ham* (1886–1924) was the richest Chinese businessman in the Indies. Starting from opium, he traded in many commodities.

**p. 29** *kembar-dampit:* Javanese have traditionally looked upon the birth of twins as a highly fraught event. In the past, the birth of opposite-sex twins *(kembar-dampit)* was interpreted by many as indicating that God had already destined them to marry each other. So the children were separated at birth and then reintroduced to each other at marriage. Same-sex twins did not need to be separated. But the birth of any twins imposed on their parents the obligation to sponsor a special performance of a shadow play. These performances, called *ruwatan,* still performed frequently in Java, take place during the day; the story related is the story of the birth of Lord Kala from the seed of Lord Guru, as per the "Foreshadowplay" of this novel. People believe it necessary to hold this ritual performance in order to ensure the well-being and success of children born as twins, or born in any of several other constellations of siblings (e.g., if a couple bears three children, the first and third of one sex and the second of the other, or five children, all males, etc.). Otherwise the children are at risk of "being eaten by Kala," understood to mean suffering some sort of misfortune; see Ward Keeler, "Release from Kala's Grip," *Indonesia* 54 (1992), 1–25.

**p. 29** The title *Haji* indicates that a man has made the pilgrimage to Mecca. Haji Hammam can therefore be assumed to be a relatively wealthy villager.

**p. 29** *Heiho* were paramilitary units that the Japanese started calling up in 1943 to support their efforts against the Allies.

**p. 29** *TKR* (Tentara Keamanan Rakyat) and *TNI* (Tentara Nasional Indonesia) are both acronyms of the Indonesian army, first formed as the People's Security Army (TKR) in 1945 and renamed the Indonesian National Army (TNI) in 1947.

**p. 29** *Pertiwi* is a fancy Javanese word for "earth"; Mother Pertiwi is the Javanese name for the earth goddess.

**p. 29** *Bijzondere H.I. School:* Education in the Netherlands Indies was limited in scope and highly hierarchical, stratified largely along racial lines. HIS *(Hollandsch-Inlandsche Scholen)* were first established in 1914 for Indonesian students; the medium of instruction was Malay.

**p. 29** *Magelang,* a town north of Yogyakarta, is where the officers' training school for the Dutch colonial army (KNIL) was located.

**p. 29** *Regency Office:* The colonial administration divided provinces into regencies, districts, and subdistricts.

**p. 30** *Kedu* is a region west of Yogyakarta, in Central Java. Bagelen and Kebumen are towns in Kedu.

**p. 31** *Prince Diponegoro* led a rebellion against the Dutch, the Java War, from 1825 to 1830, until his capture through Dutch treachery. He is much celebrated as an Indonesian proto-independence fighter.

**p. 31** *Bali* is an island east of Java, *Aceh* the region on the northwestern tip of Sumatra (west of Java). In both areas resistance to the Dutch was particularly vehement in the late nineteenth and early twentieth centuries.

**p. 31** *Halmahera* is an island in eastern Indonesia.

**p. 31** *Pancasila* refers to five principles of governance—belief in God, humanitarianism, unity, consultative deliberation, and social justice—formulated by President Sukarno and used as an ideological touchstone in Indonesia until the end of the New Order in 1998.

**p. 31** *Surabaya* is a port city in East Java.

**p. 31** *Yogya* is the short, familiar form of the name of the city Yogyakarta, in Central Java, which was the capital of the Republic of Indonesia during the Indonesian Revolution.

**p. 32** *Legimah, Friday Legi:* Javanese reckon days according to two different calendars: the international seven-day calendar (e.g., Friday) and a five-day market calendar (e.g., Legi). Any given conjunction of the two, such as Friday Legi, recurs once every thirty-five days. An old-fashioned, somewhat déclassé way to name people alludes to the day on which they are born, as Iin's mother's name, Legimah, does.

**p. 37** *Gatotkaca* is the name of one of the best-loved male characters in the shadow play repertoire. Able to fly, he is admired for his courage and his fighting skills, although he lacks the refined good looks of other warriors.

**p. 38** *Civil Servants' Ladies' Auxiliary* is an organization for the wives of civil servants. The status of each woman in the organization hinges on that of her husband in the bureaucracy.

**p. 39** *Pétruk* is one of the four servant clowns, much beloved in Java, who appear in all shadow play performances. Pétruk is tall and stringy-looking, with a big belly, a sunken chest, and a very long nose.

**p. 40** *Mataram* was a great Javanese kingdom of the sixteenth and seventeenth centuries. It was founded by Ki Ageng Pemanahan; his great-grandson, Sultan Agung, brought it to its greatest glory but eventually suffered major defeats at the hands of the Dutch.

**p. 41** *Merapi, Merbabu, Telomoyo, Sumbing,* and *Sindoro* all name mountains in Central Java.

**p. 41** *Borobudur-Mendut-Pawon* name great Buddhist monuments found in Central Java. They date to the ninth century c.e., when the Buddhist Sailendras ruled in the region.

**p. 41** *Goddess Sri* is the goddess of rice throughout much of Indonesia.

**p. 41** *Rice, Javanese varieties,* refers to the long-grain varieties of rice commonly used in Java. Since the 1960s, the Indonesian government has obliged farmers to plant new, shorter-grain varieties of rice that come to maturity much more quickly but are less appreciated because of their inferior taste and texture.

**p. 43** *Bendoro Raden Ayu* are Javanese aristocratic titles, and the long final name is typical of aristocratic family names.

**p. 45** *Soekarno* is the Dutch spelling of Sukarno's name. In current usage, the *oe,* pronounced "oo" in Dutch, is replaced by *u.*

## Chapter Two

The image at the beginning of this chapter is of Karno, an important and ambiguous figure in the shadow play repertoire. When his mother, Dewi Kunti, was still young, she was given a magical formula. She handled it carelessly, pronouncing it in sunlight, with the result that she became pregnant before she married. The sage who had given her the formula now helped her give birth through her ear. She abandoned the baby, who was found, was adopted, and eventually came under the protection of the Kurawa. Once married, Karno's mother bore the five Pandawa brothers, whom Karno was obliged to fight during the climactic Bratayuda war because the knightly code places loyalty to one's benefactors and superiors above ties to one's kin. Karno died at the hands of Arjuna, third of these, his half-brothers. It is one of the great ironies of Indonesian history that President Sukarno's name should closely resemble that of this complex character.

**p. 49** *Ibu Fatmawati* was the name of Sukarno's first wife. "Ibu" means "mother," but it is used as a respectful title, similar to "Mrs." in English, when speaking to and about middle-class or elite women. Javanese tend to have long names that are then abbreviated to show familiarity or affection: later in the chapter Ibu Fatmawati is refered to as "Bu Fat."

**p. 49** *Bung Hatta*'s renown as a nationalist was second only to Sukarno's both before and after Indonesia's Proclamation of Independence. He was vice-president of the country from the date of that proclamation until he resigned in 1956, but his power had already greatly diminished in the early 1950s, due to his temperamental differences with the more flamboyant, politically impulsive Sukarno.

**p. 50** *Joyoboyo* was a twelfth-century king in East Java who is purported to have prophesied that Java would be ruled for three centuries by white people, then by yellow dwarfs for the life cycle of a corn stalk, following which the era of prosperity would begin.

**p. 52** *Sutan Syahrir* was another important nationalist leader in the 1930s and 1940s. Unlike Hatta and Sukarno, he stood aloof from the occupying Japanese during World War II. He promoted parliamentary democracy and was named prime minister in 1945 but was replaced in 1947 by Amir Syarifuddin. Syahrir was Minang, that is, of Minangkabau ethnicity, from Sumatra.

**p. 54** *Garèng, Pétruk,* and *Bagong* are servant-clowns to the righteous parties in the shadow play repertoire. All misshapen and bumpkinish, they are at the same time dearly loved and also very familiar to virtually all Javanese, most of whom can identify much more readily with these low-status figures than with their exalted masters.

**p. 57** *FREEDOM* was a standard form of greeting in the revolutionary period.

## Chapter Three

The image at the beginning of the chapter is of Srikandi, a famous warrior-princess, one of several wives of the Pandawa hero Arjuna. She is known not only for her prowess as a fighter but also for her fiery temperament and her unwillingness to submit to standard Javanese rules of feminine deportment.

**p. 59** The *Java Hokokai,* or Java Service Association, was set up in 1944 to mobilize the Javanese to support the Japanese war effort. Sukarno and Hatta both served as officers in the organization.

**p. 60** The *KNIP,* or Central Indonesian National Committee, was the acting parliament of the Republic during the Revolution. Sukarno controlled its membership.

**p. 60** *Allied Elephant . . . :* In the first several months after the Japanese surrender in August 1945, confusion reigned as the Allies, the Japanese, and the Indonesian nationalists acted on conflicting—and sometimes confused—conceptions of the region's future. The Dutch hoped the Allies would help them reestablish the status quo ante. Indonesian nationalists were determined to prevent this from happening, and many Japanese officers with residual authority sympathized with them. But the latter were now formally obliged to obey the Allies' instructions. Those members of regional elites who had benefited from Dutch favoritism, meanwhile, were much less enthusiastic about ending colonial arrangements. The British, bringing in mostly Indian troops, sought to ensure the safety of European and Eurasian internees imprisoned by the Japanese while accepting the Japanese surrender. But in the process, they got caught up in much violence. Terrible bloodshed in the East Javanese city of Surabaya in November 1945 persuaded the British that they should support neither side in the struggle.

**p. 60** The *NICA,* or Netherlands Indies Civil Administration, was intended to reassert Dutch administrative control over areas wrested from the Japanese by advancing Allied forces during the war.

**p. 61** *Dutchmen . . . from piglet pale to burnt coconut sugar:* Javanese long referred to all foreigners as "Dutchmen," and the largely South Asian troops under British command were so called, as were the British themselves.

**p. 65** *BAPPENAS* is an acronym for the National Development Planning Board. *BULOG* refers to the National Logistical Supply Organization.

**p. 65** *Gambling* in the form of state-sponsored lotteries was sometimes used by New Order authorities to raise funds. But these lotteries always aroused controversy among religious figures.

**p. 65** *Monday Pon:* See note on Friday Legi in Chapter One.

**p. 69** *Lord Senopati* was the first great military leader and king of Mataram, the Central Javanese kingdom that rose to prominence in the late sixteenth and seventeenth centuries. He was the son of Ki Ageng Pemanahan and grandfather of Sultan Agung, both mentioned in Chapter One.

**p. 69** *pronounce their words a-a-a:* Final *a,* and penultimate and final *a* in open syllables, are pronounced *o* in the regional dialect of Javanese in use where the courts of Solo and Yogya are located. Although this represents a deviation from older pronunciation and from the pronunciation in all other areas where Javanese is spoken, the fact that this dialect is spoken at the court centers makes it the prestigious one, and speakers of this dialect consider the pronunciation of all other native Javanese speakers odd and uncouth. By the same token, inflation in the markers of politesse makes the pronouns in use at the courts shift through time, while those in outlying areas remain "old fashioned."

**p. 70** The *Pariyangan* region is in West Java, where Sundanese is spoken. Batak refers to a number of ethnic groups in northern Sumatra. Bataks are famous for their franker, more direct interpersonal style than that of many other Indonesians, especially Javanese. The Batak commander is presumably A. H. Nasution, who led West Java's Siliwangi Division during the Revolution.

**p. 70** *Werkudara* is the second of the five Pandawa brothers; unlike the others, he is large and crude-looking, but immensely strong. On first meeting his bride, *Arimbi,* he beat her against his thigh. She had already had a vision of him in her dreams, however, and found his treatment of her neither frightening nor painful.

**p. 78** *West Irian,* the western portion of the island of New Guinea, which had been colonized by the Dutch, was not included in the Dutch settlement with Indonesia at the end of the Revolution and became a source of much contention in the 1950s as Sukarno demanded increasingly stridently for its "return" to Indonesia.

**p. 78, n. 10** The *PKI,* or Indonesian Communist Party, came under the leadership of Musso at the time of his return from the Soviet Union in August 1948. He proceeded to fan animosity among leftists and anti-leftist Republican forces, and in September 1948 the PKI's supporters in Madiun started a premature coup. Its suppression by the army resulted in thousands of deaths and cast a long shadow over Indonesian politics for decades.

## Chapter Four

The image at the beginning of this chapter shows Kenyawandu. She is usually identified as an ogress but her name and features of her costume indicate that she is hermaphrodite (understood in Java to be neither male nor female). The breast cloth covers female breasts, but the clothes on the lower part of her body are masculine, and the name is made up of the Javanese words for "maiden" and "hermaphrodite." In performance, this puppet is used as a generic ogress and is given many different names.

**p. 84** *Liberal democracy,* or parliamentary democracy, disappointed many Indonesians in the course of the 1950s, as they saw a rapid turnover in governments and increasing political conflict. Finally, in 1957, it ended when martial law was declared. Sukarno then set about formulating

"Guided Democracy," an eclectic mix of grand oratory and crisis management with no real ideological coherence. Despite that lack of clear consistency, Sukarno did pronounce upon its contents in the "Political Manifesto" he formulated in his Independence Day speech of 1959.

**p. 84**   *manifespolantinekolimpronefos: nekolim* was an acronym Sukarno used to refer to the Neocolonialist, Colonialist and Imperialist forces he believed still to be seeking control over Indonesia in a worldwide struggle among Old Established Forces *(oldefos)* and New Emerging Forces *(nefos)*. Sukarno's anti-American rhetoric often reached remarkable stridency, understandable perhaps in light of American covert support to rebels in outlying islands in the 1950s.

**p. 84**   The *MPR* (People's Deliberative Assembly) was intended to meet once every five years, according to the 1945 Constitution, to elect the president and set national policy. Sukarno did not convene it until 1959, however, and then only in modified form, which he called the *MPRS* (Provisional People's Deliberative Assembly).

**p. 84**   The *Provisional People's Deliberative Assembly* meets once every five years to elect the president. It was first convened by Sukarno in 1959.

**p. 85**   *Aidit* led the Indonesian Communist Party from 1951 until he was killed, along with other leftists and people accused of leftist sympathies, in the civic upheaval of 1965–66, when the military and young men, many of them particularly devout Muslims, took the law into their own hands and murdered hundreds of thousands of their fellow citizens. The stories spread by the New Order about Aidit's death belittle him as a coward, but there is no way to know what actually took place. (*Green shirts* were worn by regular army personnel; *striped shirts* were worn by military special forces.) Klaten, a city in Central Java, saw some fighting: it was one of the few places in which politically compromised people made any effort to defend themselves. In Central and East Java, Bali, and West Sumatra, where the Communist Party was strongest and most of the violence took place, people were for the most part too stunned or overpowered to resist. Following the massacres, and the solidification of Suharto's and the military's rule, economic growth became the rationale for all government action, replacing Sukarno's grander populist and anti-imperialist themes, and birth control first received governmental approval.

**p. 86** *Aurat* refers in Arabic to the portion of the body that according to Islam must always be hidden.

**p. 86** *Lekra* was an acronym for the Institute of People's Culture, an organization affiliated with the Communist Party of Indonesia. Its members engaged in vehement polemics in the 1950s and especially the early 1960s, promoting socialist realism and excoriating artists they accused of self-indulgent "universal humanist" ruminations.

**p. 87** *Javacentric* and other adjectives derived from the word for Javanese are used in Indonesian to describe anyone who appears loyal to conservative ideas about hierarchy and enjoins people in subordinate positions to submit meekly to authority.

**p. 87** *Beijing:* The Communist Party of Indonesia followed Sukarno's lead in the early 1960s in its increasingly cordial attitude toward Communist China. *Sabang* and the other names that follow are all place names from far-flung islands of Indonesia.

**p. 88** *Bratayuda* refers to the great war that brings the conflict between the Pandawa and Kurawa cousins to its climax in the *Mahabharata.* *Arjuna* is the handsomest of the Pandawa, renowned for his amorous adventures—much as was Sukarno.

**p. 90** *Uma* is an alternate name for Umayi. *Sarpakenaka* is the sister of *Rahwana,* the evil King of Langka who kidnaps Rama's wife, *Sinta,* the paragon of feminine virtue, in the *Ramayana. Yudhistira,* the eldest of the five Pandawa brothers in the *Mahabharata,* contrasts with his younger siblings by virtue of both his absolute integrity and a modesty that borders on timidity or even weakness. The shadow play characters *Limbuk* and *Cangik* are both female servants, one skinny, the other very stout, whose gossipy exchanges afford puppeteers opportunities for comedy.

**p. 91** The *Crocodile Hole Incident* refers to the night of September 30/ October 1, 1965, when the bodies of six murdered Indonesian generals were thrown into a well, called the Crocodile Hole, at Halim Air Force Base, during the abortive coup attempt.

**p. 91** *Belief System:* The Indonesian state posits belief in God as one of the five principles of the nation (as enshrined in the Pancasila), and every citizen must declare a religious affiliation. Difficulties have arisen as to what constitutes an officially recognized religion. Suharto's New Order eventually acknowledged "belief systems" as a valid alternative to the world religions, largely to accommodate Javanese mystical beliefs that many Muslims would not accept as orthodox.

**p. 91** *aji kaluwih . . . :* The words are Javanese, and the phrase strings together words much used among Javanese mystical organizations, such as Pangestu and Sumarah, which tend toward a bland theosophical moralizing.

**p. 91** *Puncak* is a hill station south of Jakarta where wealthy residents of the city seek relief from the heat and oppressive humidity.

**p. 92** *Batam Island* faces the extraordinarily wealthy city-state of Singapore, one of the world's most important business centers. The Indonesian government has tried at various times to develop Batam both as a port and as an industrial zone, in order to take advantage of and compete with Singapore.

**p. 94** *Kartini* was the daughter of a Javanese aristocrat (a Regent in the Dutch colonial administration). She died in childbirth in 1905, only in her mid-twenties. Her writings (in Dutch), particularly letters she wrote to a Dutch correspondent, are taken as the touchstone for feminist thinking in Indonesia. But the Indonesian government has been careful to memorialize her as the epitome of refined Javanese womanhood, downplaying any critique of women's traditional roles that might be based on her writings or her biography.

**p. 95** *une celebrité:* At many points in the novel, but particularly in this chapter and the next, a number of foreign words and phrases appear. Many of them are incorrect: misspelled, ungrammatical, or otherwise faulty. These errors may be inadvertent. Or Mangunwijaya may have wished to imitate the way elite Indonesians sprinkle their speech with foreign expressions they do not completely control.

**p. 97** *W.J.S. Poerwadarminta* was the great lexicographer of Javanese and Indonesian; his dictionary of Indonesian was the standard for many years.

**p. 100** The *Round Table Conference* took place in 1949 among Dutch and Indonesian representatives in order to arrange for Indonesia's independence from the Netherlands. One of the issues it failed to settle, however, was the status of West Irian (see below).

**p. 100** The *PRRI-Permesta uprising* actually consisted of two challenges to Jakarta's authority, one (PRRI) originating in Sumatra in late 1956 and the other (Permesta) in Sulawesi in 1957, that eventually joined together. Both expressed many Outer Islanders' resentment toward the Javanese-controlled central government. By 1958 the two movements had been effectively quashed.

**p. 100** *West Irian,* the western portion of the island of New Guinea claimed by the Dutch, was not ceded by the Netherlands to Indonesia at the end of the Indonesian Revolution. Sukarno chose to foment popular fervor in the cause of winning sovereignty over the region, especially in the increasingly politically tense years of the early 1960s. The Dutch finally gave control of West Irian to the UN in 1962, and the area came under Indonesian control the following year.

## Chapter Five

The image at the beginning of this chapter is of Arjuna, handsomest and most idealized of the five Pandawa brothers in the *Mahabharata*.

**p. 104** *Nha rak tenan . . . :* "Yeah, just like I thought, you're a thief through and through, a heart-stealer, you fucking bastard!" Unlike the case of the preceding phrases in French and English, Mangunwijaya provides no translation for this phrase, which is in the East Javanese dialect of Javanese.

**p. 108** *Confrontation with Malaysia* was Sukarno's response, in 1963, to the creation of Malaysia out of Britain's former colonies, Malaya, Singapore, and Sarawak and Sabah (two regions of northern Borneo). Sukarno objected to this federation as a manifestation of Britain's neo-colonial designs and promised to crush it—in part to keep popular excitement high after the successful wresting of West Irian from the Dutch. Some military actions on Borneo in 1964, however, proved embarrassing failures.

**p. 108** *G-30S* refers to the supposed "30th September Movement," held responsible by the New Order for the failed coup of September 30, 1965. Just how large a movement this actually was has never become clear. But Suharto and his allies capitalized on the event to strip their opponents of all civil rights. Anyone wishing to gain admission to a state-run school or to gain a civil service job or to obtain any official document was obliged to provide a document proving that he or she was not implicated in this "movement." Getting such a document from one's local authorities was not always straightforward, and the requirement made many people vulnerable to corrupt demands.

**p. 109** *Gerwani,* the Indonesian Women's Movement, promoted women's rights in the 1950s and 1960s, all the while developing close links with the Indonesian Communist Party. The New Order vilified the organization and fabricated sensational charges that women who were members of the organization tortured and mutilated the bodies of the generals killed on the night of September 30, 1965.

**p. 110** *Bantul* is a town southwest of Yogyakarta.

**p. 110** *Emping crackers* are a particularly delicious but relatively expensive Javanese snack.

**p. 110** *Batik cloth* and *surjan shirts* have long been the traditional clothes worn by members of the royal courts in Yogyakarta. The *blangkon headgear* refers to long pieces of batik cloth elaborately folded and sewn into ready-made hats, to replace the simpler folded headcloths Javanese men have traditionally worn.

**p. 111** *Daendels* was governor-general of the Netherlands Indies from 1807 to 1815.

**p. 111** *Nwantara* is an old name for the Indonesian archipelago.

**p. 111** *"Hallo Hallo Bandung"* was a popular patriotic song during the period of the Revolution.

**p. 113** *Yogyakarta Hadiningrat* is a particularly elaborate name of the city, one that emphasizes its royal traditions. But the city used to be noted as well for the many horse-drawn carts that provided transport before motorized vehicles made them impractical.

**p. 114** *Rohadi couldn't pronounce* t: Most speakers of Indonesian learn a regional language before they learn Indonesian, and the way they pronounce the latter is always shaped by the former. Because Javanese are the dominant ethnic group in Indonesia, they consider their pronunci-

ation of Indonesian to be the standard. But Javanese has two different
*t* sounds, one dental (with the tip of the tongue placed behind the front
teeth) and one palatal (with the tip of the tongue touching the roof of
the mouth). When Javanese speak Indonesian, they use the dental *t*. Balinese has only one *t* sound, an alveolar one (with the tip of the tongue
placed behind the upper front teeth), and they use this sound when they
speak Indonesian, causing Javanese to marvel at the "inability" of Balinese to pronounce their *t*'s properly. For many of the same reasons,
Javanese and Balinese also pronounce *d* differently. An English speaker
might hear someone pronouncing *t* as *th* and *s* as *z* as similarly odd, so
I have rendered the contrasts by using this device.

**p. 115** *Serimpi dancers* are female dancers at the Javanese courts who
dance subtle and extremely refined dances.

**p. 116** *King Dasamuka* is another name for Rahwana in the *Ramayana*.

**p. 118** *Jagad gede jagad cilik* refers in Javanese mysticism to the macro-
cosm and microcosm, the universe beyond us and the universe within
each of us, between which the everyday world of *ngarcapada* is located.

**p. 120** *Mother Pertiwi* is the way Javanese mythology labels Mother Earth.

**p. 120** *Halim Airport* was an air force base in Jakarta.

**p. 120** The *Fifth Force* was to consist of armed workers and peasants,
as proposed by the Communist Party, counterbalancing the largely
antileftist military.

**p. 121** *Council of Generals' secrets:* Rumors abounded in Indonesia starting in the middle of 1965 that the military's top generals were planning
to oust Sukarno, whose leftist sympathies and economic mismanage-
ment they found increasingly unacceptable. Many thought the coup
would be timed to coincide with Armed Forces Day, that is, October 5.
It is possible that the move against the generals on the night of September

30 was intended to stave off Sukarno's removal from power, although it is not clear whether the rumors had any basis in fact.

**pp. 121–22** *Mistress Nyai Roro Kidul* is the goddess of the South Sea, with whom each succeeding Sultan of Yogyakarta is thought to have amorous relations. *Pétruk,* one of the servant clowns in service to the righteous party in any shadow play performance, is usually identified as a Javanese everyman. Mt. Merapi is the lone volcano that looms over Yogyakarta. It is still active and occasionally causes considerable damage to areas north of the city. *Tanjung Priok* is the bay along which the city of Jakarta originally grew, while *Kramat Raya* is one of the city's neighborhoods.

## Chapter Six

The image at the beginning of this chapter is of Togog, another of the misshapen servant clowns in the shadow play repertoire, but one who serves the evil-intentioned party, such as the evil Rahwana in the *Ramayana,* or the Kurawa in the *Mahabharata.* Togog usually sees the folly of his masters' ways but is unable, despite his best efforts, to dissuade them from embarking on foolhardy plans to mount expeditions against their rivals.

**p. 125** *Halim Air Field* in Jakarta, where Sukarno was conferring with the Communist leader Aidit at the time of the coup attempt, was where the perpetrators took the bodies of the three generals already killed, and the three other generals and one adjutant they had taken alive but then murdered at Halim early in the morning of October 1.

**p. 125** *Deputy Prime Minister Soebandrio* also served as Sukarno's Foreign Minister and was one of the most left-leaning members of Sukarno's cabinet in the 1960s.

**p. 126** *a little ripple on the surface of the ocean:* Sukarno is said to have made this dismissive remark about the murder of the six generals.

**p. 126** *Cakrabirawa* was the name of the presidential palace guard in Jakarta. Its head, Lieutenant-Colonel Untung, led the ill-fated coup attempt of September 30, 1965.

**p. 126** The *DPRGR (Dewan Perwakilan Rakyat–Gotong Royong),* or *Mutual Assistance People's Representative Council:* The People's Representative Council is Indonesia's legislative body, statutorily subordinated to the People's Deliberative Assembly (MPR), which meets only once every five years. Sukarno suspended the Council in 1960 and replaced it with the Mutual Assistance People's Representative Council (DPRGR) appointed by him.

**p. 127** *March 11, 1966, Supersemar Day:* From the time he put a stop to the coup attempt in early October 1965, Suharto started maneuvering to oust the still-popular Sukarno from the presidency. Taking advantage of street demonstrations the army had actually encouraged, Suharto pressured Sukarno into signing a letter in which he, Sukarno, "requested" that Suharto take charge. The document, the Executive Order of March 11, 1966, was called by a clever acronym, "Supersemar," incorporating the name of Semar, one of the servant clowns in shadow plays, who is also thought of as the guardian spirit of Java.

**p. 128** *Wirogunan* is the name of a prison in the city of Yogyakarta; *Kambangan Island,* just off the southern coast of West Java, is the site of another prison; the *island a long way from Java* is the island of Buru, where, starting in 1969, thousands of political prisoners were sent to hard-labor camps.

**p. 128** *Revolutionary Councils:* On the morning of October 1, 1965, a radio announcement informed the populace that generals planning a coup against Sukarno had been arrested and that Revolutionary Councils were to be formed to safeguard Sukarno's policies.

**p. 129** The *Extraordinary Military Tribunal* brought people accused of collaborating in the coup to trial, starting in 1966 and continuing until 1978.

**p. 129** *G-30S* is an acronym for the September 30 Movement *(Gerakan September 30).* *Gestok* is an acronym for the October 1 Movement *(Gerakan Satu Oktober).*

**p. 130** *watchmen's rounds:* Urban neighborhoods in Java organize nightly rounds for male residents to ensure safety and order.

**p. 131** *MULO,* or Broader Lower Education schools, were set up by the Dutch in 1914 as lower-level secondary schools.

**p. 133** *Halim Airport then Cengkareng:* Halim served as Jakarta's major airport for several years, but was then replaced by the much larger Soekarno-Hatta International Airport in Cengkareng, west of Jakarta.

**p. 135** *HIS, CGMI, IPPI:* A great many organizations flourished during the later Sukarno years, and many of them had links to the Communist Party of Indonesia, although not all members of an organization were aware of those links. Aware or not, their members found themselves politically compromised once anyone suspected of leftist sympathies became open to arrest, imprisonment or execution following the New Order's establishment in 1965.

**p. 140** *taking unilateral action:* In late 1963 and 1964, the Communist Party tried, primarily through the Indonesian Peasants' Front, to implement provisions of the land reform law passed in 1960 by taking "unilateral actions" against landowners in East Java. These actions led to violent conflicts, resulting in few gains for the poor but greatly increased tensions between the Communist Party and its opponents.

**p. 140** *Going down to the masses* is a still-current phrase used by educated Indonesians to describe associating with the poor or rural population.

**p. 142** *Transmigration* is a policy, first instituted by the Dutch at the start of the twentieth century and supported with ever-greater enthusiasm by Sukarno and then Suharto, whereby people from the densely populated islands of Java, Madura, Bali and Lombok are moved to the more sparsely populated Outer Islands. Some people have experienced such a move as a boon; many others have resisted going or become disenchanted once they have moved. Often people living in the way of development projects have been officially encouraged, and/or unofficially pressured, to transmigrate. Some of the recent ethnic tensions in Indonesia have been exacerbated by transmigration projects.

**p. 147** *Communist Party member or OK-EM:* Every Indonesian citizen is obliged to carry an identity card. The threat of labeling someone as a leftist on his or her identity card was an effective ploy to keep people in line throughout the New Order years.

## Chapter Seven

The image at the beginning of this chapter is of a *raseski,* a generic female giant demon.

**p. 149** *Goddess Sri's chamber* is a small room in Javanese houses where the household's store of rice is kept. Sri is the goddess of rice and of fertility. Newlyweds sleep in a room next to it in order to be assured both privacy and fertility.

**p. 152** *duh Gusti:* The phrase is in Javanese, specifically the self-humbling Javanese that people use when speaking to superiors. It is a standard invocation of God; in this case, it expresses astonishment and gratitude.

**p. 153** *Ronggowarsito* was the last of the great classical Javanese poets. Few Javanese now read his works; in the popular imagination he is renowned primarily for his reputed mystical foreknowledge of Java's history. *Queen Kencana Wungu* was a queen of Majapahit, the great fourteenth-century Hindu-Javanese kingdom.

**p. 155** *Air Force General Omar Dhani* and Deputy Prime Minister Soebandrio were among the many high-ranking officials associated with leftist politics who were tried by the Extraordinary Military Tribunal in Jakarta following the September 30 coup. Although both were sentenced to death, only Omar Dhani was killed.

**p. 156** *National Resurgence Day* is a holiday celebrated on May 20 every year, commemorating the early nationalist movement.

**p. 156** *Senayan Stadium* in Jakarta is the site of the president's annual Independence Day speech. Sukarno gave some of his most memorable addresses there. Suharto's speeches never aroused much excitement, there or elsewhere.

**p. 159** *Queen Banowati:* See the note on the image at the beginning of Chapter Eight.

## Chapter Eight

The image at the beginning of this chapter is of Queen Banowati. She is the wife of the eldest Kurawa, King Duryadana. But her first love was Arjuna, Duryadana's greatest enemy, and she passes up no opportunity to flirt with him, or to make invidious comparisons between him and her husband, a stunning deviation from proper wifely behavior.

**p. 163** *clean-environment lightning operation:* The New Order regime continued to take advantage of people's political vulnerability by insisting that anyone wishing to join the civil service or participate in any political activity had to prove that he or she came from a "clean environment," that is, that neither the individual nor any member of his or her family, going back two generations, was in any way implicated in leftist or other oppositional activities.

**p. 164** A *Letter of Authorization to Print* and a *Permit to Operate a Press* are both required to publish anything in Indonesia, so that the government can keep close control over what does and does not appear in print.

**p. 164** The *kayon* is a large, cone-shaped figure that is placed in the middle of the screen until a shadow play begins. The puppeteer replaces it there at the conclusion of a performance.

# Afterword: Mangunwijaya
# as Novelist / Puppeteer

On the back cover of the original Indonesian edition of *Durga / Umayi,*
Mangunwijaya is quoted as saying that the book "is epic in nature . . . ,
but in its literary form it might be called an 'anti-epic.'" No doubt
he meant by this remark to highlight the irreverent tenor of the novel,
its skewering of the grand, mythologizing rhetoric of Indonesian
nationalist history. But I suspect he was thinking of something else
as well. The word *epic* might well bring to a reader's mind the Indian
epics *Ramayana* and *Mahabharata* on which the Javanese shadow play
tradition is based. But any reader of Indonesian fiction, when asked
to name an *Indonesian* epic, would be likely to think first of Pramoedya
Ananta Toer's four-volume series the *Buru Quartet,* written while
Pramoedya was a political prisoner held on Buru Island (the island
where Iin's lover dies in Chapter Five of *Durga / Umayi*). Pramoedya
is Indonesia's only contemporary writer with an international reputation, one based largely on that imposing set of four novels. If we
take Mangunwijaya's remark as a sly allusion to Pramoedya's mag-
num opus, then he is encouraging us to compare the particular qualities of Pramoedya's and his own fictional renderings of Indonesian
history.

The first three volumes of the *Buru Quartet* relate in a first-person
narrative a young Javanese man's sentimental education—starting
from when he falls in love with and marries a beautiful Eurasian
woman named Annelies—an education that proceeds in parallel with
his political awakening. His passage to nationalist awareness is

hardly simple or straightforward. He must overcome his uncritical awe of all things Dutch. An aristocrat, he must overcome that class's unthinking arrogance; highly educated and fluent in Dutch, he must overcome his contempt for the languages, both Javanese and Malay, that most people around him use. At the same time, he must learn to distinguish between exploitative foreigners, on the one hand, and sympathetic and progressive ones, on the other; he must avoid ethnic stereotypes and mindless cultural pride; he must develop organizational and political skills that transcend local rivalries and forge larger, more powerful solidarities. Above all, he must come to understand the democratic and egalitarian ideals of modern nationalist states and promote them over both colonial exploitation and nativist narrow-mindedness. The fourth volume takes a radically different turn: the narrative voice passes to a collaborator, an indigenous functionary in the colonial administration who tracks every move of this dangerously clear-headed nationalist figure—and who, at once personally corrupt but admiring of his prey, destroys himself even as he observes and abets the decline of his nemesis.

Magnificent in its complexity and filled with dramatic incidents (particularly in the first two volumes), Pramoedya's tetralogy has a high-minded seriousness that seems only appropriate to the magnitude of its subject matter: how an individual, and a people, must struggle to sort out the gains and the evils of the colonial experience and thereby strive toward a just and progressive modernity. Pramoedya was a famous leftist author and intellectual in Indonesia in the 1950s and 1960s, before his imprisonment, and he studied the past assiduously. But in writing his epic, he certainly intended not just to remind Indonesians of their history, but also to make clear how thoroughly the New Order regime had betrayed the nationalists' original, or best, intentions. The New Order's leaders knew perfectly well what Pramoedya was about and banned each of the four volumes in turn; only after Suharto fell in 1998 was the ban lifted.

The *Buru Quartet* ends before either Sukarno's rise to prominence or Indonesian independence appeared likely, and Pramoedya's hero, Minke, dies before Mangunwijaya's heroine—if she deserves the label—is born. But by picking up the thread of Indonesia's history and following it through to the proclamation of independence and beyond, *Durga/Umayi* fills us in on what the great nationalist struggle has led to. And in tandem with the shift of attention from Indonesia's proto-independence to its post-independence era, Mangunwijaya makes a dramatic shift in tone. He sets his "anti-epic" apart from Pramoedya's epic above all by transposing Pramoedya's high-toned fictionalized history into a mercurial, comic fantasy, at times bitter, at times poignant, but never, ever grand.

The shift in tone is essential because the elevated style cannot convey anything like lived experience, certainly not the lived experience of the fallible, unheroic sorts of characters whose stories Mangunwijaya wishes to tell. Indeed, Pramoedya's novels, while fascinating and deeply compelling, are written in a highly literary style that makes dialogue among his characters somewhat stilted. Pramoedya may have wanted to remind his readers that many of his characters' conversations would not have taken place in Indonesian or Javanese at all but rather in Dutch. But his language rarely gives up a certain formality, *gravitas* even, that bespeaks his story's historic stature. That Pramoedya's inspiration comes from the tradition of the novel rather than from any Indonesian performance genre is apparent in the lack of comedy in the tetralogy: in Java and Bali, at least, few are the performances that let the serious nature of a story rule out opportunities for comic horseplay among low-status characters.

Mangunwijaya is happy to create an absurdly cosmopolitan Indonesian in this novel. But by making shadow plays a model for his narrative, he arrives at a brilliant solution to the problem of how to make the language sound likely, and how to make his characters inhabit a world that is at once fantastic and highly familiar. Like any Javanese performance genre, furthermore, his novel mixes tragedy and farce with complete nonchalance.

How much Mangunwijaya wished to evoke shadow plays in the novel became particularly clear at a conference he participated in at Sydney University in 1998. It was uncertain until the last minute whether he would be able to attend the gathering, which concerned postcolonial studies and modern Indonesian literature.[1] Suharto had finally responded to immense popular pressure and left office just a few days before the conference was scheduled to begin, and Mangunwijaya was in the thick of the protests and discussions taking place in Jakarta at the time. At last the conference organizers, Tony Day and Keith Foulcher, received word that Father Mangun would indeed come, although he would have to leave the conference early in order to reach Jakarta in time for a scheduled meeting with Suharto's replacement, Habibi.

When Father Mangun's turn came to make a presentation at the conference, he chose to read two excerpts from his novel *Durga / Umayi.* First he read the *Prawayang* ("Foreshadowplay"), and then he read the portion of the second chapter (starting from the sentence I have translated "So when the sun finally rose on the long-awaited day . . .") that describes Sukarno proclaiming Indonesian independence on August 17, 1945. Remarkably, rather than read in a conversational style as one might expect from so much of the writing, Mangunwijaya almost intoned the passages. In so doing, he emphasized the affinities between the novel he had written and the shadow play tradition that the novel invokes, and the affinities between his role as novelist and the role of the shadow puppeteer.

A puppeteer speaks almost continuously throughout an eight-

---

1. Several of the conference participants' essays have been published in Keith Foulcher and Tony Day, eds., *Clearing a Space: Postcolonial Readings of Modern Indonesian Literature* (Leiden: KITLV Press, 2002). My contribution to the volume, "The Postcolonialist Dilemma," considers Pramoedya's, Mangunwijaya's, and Westerners' attitudes toward hierarchy.

or nine-hour performance, but he never speaks in an everyday voice. Instead, he takes on a great array of different voices, those of all the characters in the play. Even when he speaks as the narrator rather than for a character, a puppeteer does so in a highly stylized voice, one that any Javanese instantly recognizes as a puppeteer's. It was this narrator's voice that Father Mangun chose to take on as he read from his novel. Word-play is pervasive in any puppeteer's delivery as narrator: he strings together words that have the same meaning but are taken from Sanskrit or Old Javanese or other obscure sources, and / or words and phrases that rhyme or otherwise resonate with each other. Mangunwijaya does the same whenever he writes in a narrator's voice in the novel, delightedly playing with sound as he weaves words into long phrases, richly mixing assonance, rhythmic patterns, punning, and rhymes.

When Javanese list the qualities by which a puppeteer is judged, the trait they usually deem most important is the puppeteer's ability to differentiate characters' speech—the sound, pitch, speed, and timbre of their voices, in addition to the sorts of things they might say. For the best-known characters, people have clear ideas of exactly how each one should sound. For other characters, expectations are less specific, but there are still generic constraints about what an ogre, or a knight, or a demure female, or a servant should sound like and what sentiments each should express. It is because many puppeteers are so effective at differentiating voices that millions of people in Java listen to radio broadcasts of shadow plays and can follow who's speaking simply by the sound of "their" voices.

So an obvious affinity between the tradition and this novel is the precision with which Mangunwijaya reproduces the idiom of people's speaking and thinking. With barely a quotation mark in the entire text, Mangunwijaya cues his readers as to who is speaking when by rendering each character's tone—whether obsequious (e.g., the village official in Chapter Six) or puzzled yet resigned (Iin's auntie at the end of Chapter Two) or self-righteously but disingenuously angry (Iin's response to the journalist in Chapter Four) or affable yet anxious (the neighborhood head in Chapter Six), etc., etc.—with great acuteness.

Of course, a novelist, like a puppeteer, is often evaluated for the ability to get speech right, to have an ear for ways particular people at particular times might express themselves. But novelists are not supposed to traffic in stereotypes: it is the ability to create rounded, unique individuals that usually wins a novelist praise. Pramoedya's main character in the *Buru Quartet,* Minke, is a strongly delineated, because unusual and complex, character. Some of his other characters, particularly female ones, strike many readers as highly improbable. His first wife, Annelies, seems awfully pale, while her mother, Nyai Ontosoroh, seems impossibly capable.[2] Yet they, too, and several secondary characters as well, have clear identities. They are not easily forgotten, and many scenes in the tetralogy have great dramatic power as various personalities come into conflict with one another.

As I noted in the Introduction, the characters in Mangunwijaya's novel are stereotypes—the village bumpkin, the wheeling and dealing bourgeoise, the reckless youth, etc.—but they are still both vivid and affecting. One reason for that vividness is that we so often hear their speech and have no trouble imagining them on the basis of that speech. But another reason is that Mangunwijaya, in addition to getting their speech right, also empathizes deeply with them, that is, with ordinary, unheroic, morally compromised people who have had to deal with ordinary, unheroic, and morally compromising post-Independence Indonesia, often with horrifying results.

Perhaps Mangunwijaya's single most impressive accomplishment

---

2.  See Tineke Hellwig, *In the Shadow of Change: Images of Women in Indonesian Literature* (Berkeley: University of California Centers for South and Southeast Asian Studies, 1994).

is indeed the sympathy he evinces for all of the characters in the novel, even as they engage in practices—gun-running, smuggling, prostitution, deception, self-promotion—we can only condemn. The conditions in which modern Indonesians find themselves arouses Mangunwijaya's outrage, but the binds in which Indonesia's citizens find themselves arouse his unstinting compassion. To retell Indonesian history with such an unblinking eye for its moral heedlessness, corruption, and tragedy, yet refrain from ever treating the novel's characters with condescension or contempt, moves the novel beyond any usual political satire to something much more complex and affecting. *Durga/Umayi* is as a result scathing, funny, and quick, but it is also surprisingly, and deeply, moving.

The moment in Chapter Six, to take one example, when Iin is confronted with the unintended consequences of her mixing radical political activities with romantic pleasure—that they have brought about Rohadi's imprisonment—is masterfully rendered. The long stretch during which we hear the neighborhood head's words but are told nothing about Iin's reaction (evocative of Aeneas's lame excuses to a silent Dido in Book 4 of the *Aeneid*) splits our attention between the speaker who is unaware of his words' impact and a listener who is undergoing excruciating but unspoken pain. This sudden discovery of responsibility for things one had given little or no thought to, the realization of one's own complicity in terrible events, recurs at several points in the novel. Iin realizes too late that she has condemned her own brother to forcible removal from the land in Chapter Seven, and once again she attains belated awareness of the fruits of her own heedlessness. This time we watch Iin raging at herself—but from the perspective of uncomprehending villagers. The hapless nature of corruption and tragedy comes through in this way: in New Order Indonesia, the wrecking of people's lives takes place as much unthinkingly as maliciously, although no less tragically for all that.

A woman, an opportunist, and in some respects a moral mon-

ster, Iin contrasts with her creator particularly greatly. Yet she more
than any other character earns our sympathy. And for all the fantastic elements in her life course, she comes to seem more believable
than any of Pramoedya's female characters in the *Buru Quartet*. Indeed,
the novel articulates a thoughtful feminist perspective, an unusually
cogent one in recent Indonesian fiction, since we are reminded at
many points that Iin's actions stem from her refusal to accept the
subordinate role her gender would normally impose on her. She is
outraged at the difference between her brother's liberty and her cease-
less chores during their childhood, and she is never ready to settle
into conventional feminine propriety as an adult. Gang rape is shown
to have indelible consequences on her thoughts: the sensitivity with
which Mangunwijaya handles this issue is remarkable.[3]

  A question then presents itself: How did Mangunwijaya come
by his remarkable empathy for people who may have shared his
provincial origins but were actually very much unlike him? Father
Mangun, after all, was not only remarkably accomplished; he was
also remarkably, even fearlessly, principled, and that in a society, New
Order Indonesia, in which very few people could not be intimidated
and / or bribed into acquiescence.

  As a Roman Catholic priest in a society whose population is over-
whelmingly Muslim, Mangunwijaya was a marginal and even anom-
alous figure in Java. But for that very reason, he was able to fulfill a
venerable Javanese role, that of the ascetic sage who lives apart from
the center of power and can therefore observe it more critically and
dispassionately than those caught up in its machinations. The New
Order regime, controlled largely by Indonesians of Javanese descent,
tolerated him because, as a Catholic, he could never develop any

---

3.  For a more critical reading of Mangunwijaya's treatment of feminist
    issues, see Michael Bodden's essay "Woman as Nation in Mangunwi-
    jaya's *Durga Umayi,*" *Indonesia* 62 (October 1996), 53–82.

power base, and because, as a holy man, his mistreatment would only bring shame on the government. The end result was that he was looked upon by a great many people as a uniquely courageous public figure and champion of the poor. That Father Mangun was able to imagine himself in the mind of a woman, however apparently cartoonish, with such success suggests that he felt some affinities between his own position in Javanese society and that of a poor woman of peasant stock. Both, certainly, stand at the margins of power. There is another resemblance between them as well: they are both childless in a society in which having children marks the line between minority and social maturity.

Mangunwijaya is perfectly forthright on the subject of sex. He sees that sex presents women with a powerful option when they're searching for strategies to make their way in the world. Sex can also be a degrading, dangerous, and loathsome means to a woman's ends, as the passage in Chapter Five in which Iin viciously mocks her johns' desires makes clear. Iin has the looks and the stamina to use sex very effectively, although she does not rely on her body alone: one reason she succeeds so well as a call girl is that she speaks fluent Dutch, and that achievement came as a result of her very shrewdly befriending two Dutch girls in Magelang in her youth. But Mangunwijaya doesn't moralize about sex: he shows its effectiveness, and its costs, when brought into play by an ambitious woman who has little going for her other than her will, her drive, and her looks.

But sex is not the same thing as parenthood. For a Javanese man or woman to marry marks the beginning of his or her passage to full status in a community, but only on the birth of a child does someone actually attain that status. Giving up sexual activity, and even giving up day-to-day social relations in order to take on an ascetic's status outside the normal world, has a venerable history in Java. But the man who chooses this path does so after he has married and sired children. To foreswear marriage and generation altogether makes no cultural sense in Java. When an American anthropologist spoke to friends in a Javanese village about a Javanese Catholic priest she knew, they were incredulous when she explained that he was not married because of the Catholic vow of celibacy. Surely, they exclaimed, she had got it wrong: no man would *choose* not to have children (Morris, personal communication). To these villagers, for a man or a woman to be childless could not be understood as anything other than a personal tragedy.

Iin's childlessness does constitute an implicit tragedy in her life. But it is not one to which she gives any thought. Her sexuality, indeed her ability to connect with others in any way, is severely affected by the experience of rape and terror early in the novel; and when she begins to heal, on meeting Rohadi, events force her to give up her body, through plastic surgery, in still more extreme ways. The fact that Iin's radical makeover takes place on the very day, March 11, 1966, that Sukarno was obliged formally to yield power to Suharto suggests that Indonesia went from the Old to the New Order by a sleight of hand, a surgical falsification that denied the nation its true origins and identity, creating a completely made-up set of appearances. Indonesian history, Mangunwijaya suggests, has subjected ordinary people to extraordinary travail, and they have come out of it scarred—while the society they live in has grown unjust, exploitative, and sterile.

For Mangunwijaya himself, the priestly tradition of celibacy was in contrast freeing. At a time when, particularly in the United States, the sexual transgressions of Catholic priests have raised fundamental questions as to whether that tradition should stand, it is worth noting how much Father Mangun's life exemplified frequently adduced justifications for the rule. Because he had no obligations to a family of his own, he was able to champion the interests of the powerless with a courage and tenacity others could not responsibly match. Poor people living along the riverbanks in downtown Yogyakarta still speak with admiration of Father Mangun, who stopped the razing of their community by moving to it himself—a smelly, crowded, and mosquito-ridden red-light district though it was—and living there for several years, until such time as he felt that the community's future was secure from "urban renewal." Many neighborhoods in Jakarta, incidentally, lacking the protection of a prominent figure like Mangunwijaya, have fallen prey to fire and destruction when politicians and developers decided urban renewal was in the public's, and their own, interests.

It is a great tragedy for contemporary Indonesia that Mangunwijaya died of a stroke shortly before his seventieth birthday, in 1999.[4] His death deprives Indonesia's public sphere of an influential and thoughtful figure at a time when the country needs many such people. But in the novel he wrote to present his reflections on Indonesia's recent history, for all the array of different voices he takes on, we can still hear his own, at once funny, indignant, and generous.

---

4. Jennifer Lindsay published an informative and moving obituary of Mangunwijaya in *Indonesia* 67 (April 1999), 201–3.

# Further Reading

Readers who would like to learn more about Indonesian society and history can pursue that interest by reading Indonesian fiction in translation, and/or nonfiction. I list some of the most notable titles in each category.

One other novel by Mangunwijaya, *The Weaverbirds,* has appeared in English (Jakarta: Lontar Press). It treats questions of divided loyalties in the early years of independent Indonesia, but in a serious style that couldn't contrast more with that of *Durga/Umayi.* Pramoedya Ananta Toer's works represent the most famous and most easily obtainable Indonesian literature translated into English. As I have suggested in my afterword, his *Buru Quartet* is a stirring account of early Indonesian nationalism and provides an interesting foil to Mangunwijaya's madcap account of what happened later. (All four volumes are published by Penguin Books; the first two volumes are the more compelling read, but taken together the four have a great cumulative impact.) Pramoedya's short stories from the 1950s, *Tales from Jakarta* (Ithaca, N.Y.: Cornell University Southeast Asia Program), are also justly famous. *The Girl from the Coast* (New York: Hyperion) is the most recent novel by Pramoedya to be made available in English. For translations of fiction by other Indonesian authors, Lontar Press is the best single resource; at the time of this writing, a list of Lontar's publications was available at http://www.lontar.org.

The scholarly literature on Indonesia is immense. I will note only a few books that relate most directly to themes touched on in

*Durga / Umayi.* An invaluable reference work, one that I have drawn on in annotating the novel, is Robert Cribb's *Historical Dictionary of Indonesia* (Metuchen, N.J.: Scarecrow Press). A concise and balanced narrative history is M. C. Ricklef's *A History of Modern Indonesia Since 1200* (Chicago: University of Chicago Press). Adam Schwarz's *A Nation in Waiting* (St. Leonards, New South Wales: Allen and Unwin) focuses specifically on later New Order Indonesia. *Indonesia Today,* edited by G. Lloyd and S. Smith (Singapore: Institute of Southeast Asian Studies), contains essays reflecting on the achievements and depredations of Indonesia's twentieth-century history and their implications for the country's future. Always insightful and provocative, Benedict Anderson has collected a number of his essays concerning Indonesia in *Language and Power* (Ithaca, N.Y.: Cornell University Press). Feminist issues in Indonesia are treated in a collection of essays edited by Laurie Sears, *Fantasizing the Feminine in Indonesia* (Durham, N.C.: Duke University Press). Among anthropological works on Java, Clifford Geertz's *Religion of Java* (Chicago: University of Chicago Press) remains essential. Robert Jay's *Javanese Villagers* (Cambridge, Mass.: MIT Press) provides a good sense of rural life. Several books describe the Javanese shadow play tradition. Victoria Clara van Groenendael's *Wayang Theatre in Indonesia* (Dordrecht: Foris Publications) provides an extensive bibliography. My *Javanese Shadow Plays, Javanese Selves* (Princeton, N.J.: Princeton University Press) analyzes the tradition with reference to Javanese ideas about self, social relations, and aesthetic pleasure.